Eight Great American Rail Journeys

A TRAVEL GUIDE

KAREN IVORY
INTRODUCTION BY JOHN GRANT

The Globe Pequot Press

Guilford, Connecticut

Cover and text design by Libby Kingsbury
Cover photo by Calvin Hall
Maps by Maryann Dube

Photo credits: pp. 2–3, 8: Randy Brandon/Third Eye Photography;
pp. 12–13, 14, 20, 64: Brian Solomon; pp. 17, 19: © NYS
Department of Economic Development; pp. 22–23, 25, 27, 28:
© Kerrick James; p. 31: Eladio Ramos Piña; pp. 32–33, 42:
American Orient Express photo by Carl and Ann Purcell; pp. 34, 38,
39: American Orient Express Photo; p. 41: National Park Service;
pp. 44–45, 46, 48, 49, 50, 52, 53: Matthew G. Wheeler; pp. 54–55,
66–67: © Amtrak; p. 58: Oregon Tourism Commission/Larry Geddis;
pp. 59, 61: © Val Flesch; p. 62: Tacoma-Pierce County Visitor &
Convention Bureau; pp. 68, 75: Georgia Department of Industry,
Trade & Tourism; p. 80: Christian Racich/WP&YR; p. 85: H.C.
Barley Collection; p. 86: John Hyde/WP&YR. All others by John
Grant.

Library of Congress Cataloging-in-Publication Data

Ivory, Karen.
   Eight great American rail journeys: a travel guide / by Karen Ivory.—1st ed.
     p. cm.
   ISBN 0–7627–0748–8
    1. United States—Tours. 2. Railroad travel—United States—Guidebooks.
    I. Title.

   E158 .I95 2000
   917.304'929—dc21

                                      00–039358

Printed in China
First Edition/First Printing

Contents

The prices and rates listed in this guidebook were
confirmed at press time. We recommend, however, that you
call establishments to obtain current information
before traveling.

Help Us Keep This Guide Up to Date

Every effort has been made by the authors and editors to make this guide as accurate and useful as possible. However, many things can change after a guide is published—establishments close, phone numbers change, and so on.

We would love to hear from you concerning your experiences with this guide and how you feel it could be made better and kept up to date. While we may not be able to respond to all comments and suggestions, we'll take them to heart and we'll make certain to share them with the authors. Please send your comments and suggestions to the following address:

The Globe Pequot Press
Reader Response/Editorial Department
P.O. Box 480
Guilford, CT 06437

Or you may e-mail us at:

editorial@globe-pequot.com

Thanks for your input, and happy travels!

Introduction

People love to talk about trains. Just get a rail fan started and the stories come quickly. They are always full of energy and emotion, a reflection of the romantic connection many people have with rail travel. Fortunately, producing television programs and writing books about train travel provides many opportunities to meet such people.

"Trains are an amazing way to see the landscape," says folklorist Nick Spitzer about his *American Orient Express* trip from New Orleans to Mobile, Alabama. "The views are all water vistas, swamp vistas, bayous, canals, and even the open Gulf on occasion. It's kind of a liquid land environment."

With train travel the going is just as important as the getting there. You see the backs of yards, the industrial sections of small and large towns, farms, and marshy swamplands. Trains provide a unique glimpse of North America, a view often missed with other types of travel.

The train journey we took to the Copper Canyon was on board the *Sierra Madre Express*. With its open-air lounge and observation area, it is a spectacular place to enjoy the beauty and spirit of the trip. "You can smell Mexico. You can hear Mexico," says *Sierra Madre Express* owner Peter Robbins with his typical enthusiasm for both the country and the train. "You're actually participating in the sights, sounds, and smells of Mexico."

To the north, on board the White Pass & Yukon Route Railroad, it is easy to imagine what it must have been like for gold-hungry stampeders passing this way more than a hundred years ago, especially on a gray, foggy morning as the train creeps up a steep grade only a few dozen yards from the original "Trail of '98."

On board a train, we can pass through small towns and vast regions nearly unnoticed. The train slips quietly into the landscape and captures the imagination. The trips described in *Eight Great American Rail Journeys* are just a starting point for the opportunities that await you on the rails. We hope you enjoy the ride.

—John Grant

The Alaska Railroad

Spectacular wilderness, North America's highest mountain, wildlife roaming free in its natural environment—these wonders await passengers on board the Alaska Railroad's Denali Star *between Anchorage and Fairbanks. Travelers who are booked on private tours may ride in more luxury in the reserved railcars pulled behind, but service for all on board the Alaska Railroad is outstanding. And the real treat here is not the train itself, but the glorious scenery that is Alaska.*

THE TRAIN
The *Denali Star*

The Alaska Railroad (AKRR) is one of the country's few remaining full-service railroads providing both passenger and freight service throughout the year. Many visitors come as part of a planned tour or cruise and travel on board the private cars that pull up the rear of the *Denali Star*. But the AKRR coaches are very comfortable, and this state-owned railroad features some of the best on-train guides and services of any railway in North America.

■ Originally constructed to haul gold from Fairbanks, the Alaska Railroad is now one of the state's top tourist attractions.

The dark blue and bright yellow cars of the AKRR are clean and well maintained. Each coach offers reclining seats with lots of legroom and large picture windows. Baggage racks extend over most seats, and shelves are provided for luggage at the rear of each car.

THE ROUTE
Anchorage ~ Wasilla ~ Talkeetna ~ Denali National Park ~ Fairbanks

The *Denali Star* makes the 356-mile trip between Alaska's two largest cities in about twelve hours. The pace is leisurely, and the train frequently slows to allow passengers a chance for a close-up view of

wildlife or to photograph a particularly scenic view of Mount McKinley. Passengers are welcome to plan their own itineraries with overnight stops along the way, the most popular being at Talkeetna and Denali National Park. The AKRR will even help make arrangements for individual itineraries, just call (800) 544–0552.

During the peak summer months, the train runs daily in both directions. The train pulls out of Anchorage early in the morning, headed for the Alaska Range, a magnificent 600-mile arc of mountains that divides south-central Alaska from the interior plateau. If the weather cooperates, passengers can catch their first glimpse of Denali (also known as Mount McKinley) less than a half-hour out of Anchorage. The route parallels the Talkeetna Mountains and the Susitna River, pulling into Talkeetna in late morning. Talkeetna is also the departure point for the AKRR's *Hurricane Turn,* one of the last flag-stop trains in North America. Leaving Talkeetna, the *Denali Star* begins a gradual climb toward the Continental Divide and an area of isolated wilderness.

Wooded areas and riverbeds along the Denali Star *route provide many opportunities to look for wildlife.*

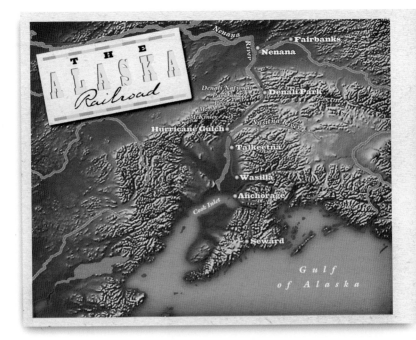

The train arrives at Denali Station in the late afternoon, and most people get off to experience the park, whether for several days or just overnight. After leaving Denali, the train enters the beautiful Nenana River canyon, traveling along rocky ledges with river views below. As the train nears Fairbanks, its route crosses the Tanana River on the 702-foot-long Mears Memorial Bridge, one of the world's longest single-span bridges.

■ Part of the Alaska Railroad parallels the Knik Arm—a cove-like body of water that has the second highest tides in the world, sometimes reaching up to 40 feet.

■ The train passes near an Eklutna Indian Village that is home to St. Nicholas Church—an 1800s log structure that is one of the oldest surviving examples of Russian architecture in North America.

RATES

The one-way fare between Anchorage and Fairbanks during the peak summer season is $160; value fare during May and September is $128. The train will make arrangements for those wanting to spend the night in Denali.

WHAT'S INCLUDED: The Alaska Railroad offers free baggage checking, as passengers are allowed only one carry-on each.

WHAT'S NOT INCLUDED: A special handling fee of $20 applies to oversized bags, overweight bags, golf bags, camping equipment, and bicycles. Onboard food and gratuities are extra.

ON BOARD

DINING: The *Denali Star*'s diner cars offer a casual and relaxed atmosphere. Meals are available throughout the trip and no reservations are required. All food is prepared onboard. Entrees feature an Alaskan twist, with such items as the McKinley Breakfast, Bristol Bay Grill, and the Indian River Sandwich, made with reindeer sausage. A cafe car offers light snacks and beverages.

DRESS CODE: The dress code on the *Denali Star* should be determined by what side activities are planned. More strenuous outdoor activities like backpacking or mountaineering in Denali National Park would obviously require special gear.

PASSENGERS: Because most of the people who ride the *Denali*  *Star* are there as part of a vacation, the atmosphere on board is that of a relaxed group sharing an adventure.

CREW: The crew is helpful and friendly. The railroad also takes pride in training and employing selected local students to serve as tour guides during the peak summer season. The students are well prepared by way of a special training class that emphasizes the history of the railroad and points of interest along the way.

MAJOR STOPS

■ **ANCHORAGE:** Visitors interested in exploring Anchorage should stop at the **Log Cabin Visitors Center** (corner of Fourth Avenue and F Street; 907–274–3531) for a visitors guide and a map for a self-guided tour. **The Anchorage Museum of History and Art** (121 West Seventh Avenue; 907–343–4326) offers a wonderful opportunity to get a quick history of Alaskan explorers; life-size dioramas depict Alaskan habitats. Of interest to rail buffs is the **Potter Section House,** 7 miles south of Anchorage. It is the only section house built on the rail line that survives at its original location. The house is now a small railroad museum. It also serves as headquarters for **Chugach State Park,** a 495,000-acre wilderness area ideal for hiking or watching wildlife (907–345–5014).

HIGHLIGHT

■ *Mount McKinley is the crown jewel of the Alaska Range. The State of Alaska officially refers to McKinley by its Tanaina Indian name, Denali, which means "the high one." In 1896 a gold prospector named it for then-President William McKinley, a political act to oppose those who wanted a silver dollar standard. From the top of McKinley, you can see for 250 miles—farther than from any mountain in the world, even Everest, which is obscured by other Himalayan peaks. First conquered in 1910, about 1,000 people attempt to climb McKinley each year, most in June.*

There are many lodging options for travelers wishing to spend some time in Anchorage prior to boarding the train. The **Clarion Suites Hotel Anchorage** at 325 West Eighth Avenue (907–274–1000) is within walking distance of the Alaska Railroad. Centrally located between the airport and the railroad is **A Wildflower Inn** (1239 I Street; 907–274–1239), a bed and breakfast furnished with antiques and featherbeds. The **Anchorage International Airport** (907–266–2525) is located about 6 miles from downtown.

■ Built in 1921 from the sides working inward, the Hurricane Gulch Bridge provides one of the route's most scenic viewpoints.

■ AKRR's *Hurricane Turn* is one of the last flag-stop trains in North America, making random stops along the way to drop off food and supplies to people who live in isolated areas.

■ **WASILLA:** Although the *Denali Star's* first stop is Wasilla, travelers who want to explore this quaint Alaskan town should consider making a separate day trip from Anchorage. Just an hour-and-a-half drive north of Anchorage, Wasilla is the headquarters of the **Iditarod sled dog race,** a grueling 1,100-mile annual race from Anchorage to Nome that takes the mushers over two mountain ranges in an average of eleven days. The headquarters at Knik-Goose Bay Road is open year-round, and includes exhibits on the history of the Iditarod, as well as notable dogs and mushers (907–376–5155; www.iditarod.com).

The **Museum of Alaska Transportation and Industry** located just north of town (P.O. Box 870646, Wasilla, AK 99687; 907–376–1211) tells the stories of the people and the machines that opened

Alaska to exploration and growth.

There are several **bed and breakfasts** available in the Wasilla area, including: **Yukon Don's** (1830 East Parks Highway #386, 2221 Yukon Circle; 800–478–7472; www.yukondon.com); and the **Agate Inn** (4725 Begich Circle; 800–770–2290; www.agateinn.com).

■ **TALKEETNA:** A genuine Alaska frontier town, Talkeetna serves as the initial base camp for climbers attempting Mount McKinley. The town also offers flightseeing adventures, world-class salmon fishing, rafting, and boating excursions. This community of about 600 residents is located at the confluence of the Susitna, Chulitna, and Talkeetna Rivers. Listed on the National Register of Historic Places, Talkeetna's streets are lined with older buildings housing museums, taverns, shops, and B&Bs.

Although many private companies offer excursions, the **Talkeetna Denali Visitors Center** serves as a clearinghouse for information on local activities and provides booking services (P.O. Box 688, Talkeetna, AK 99676; 800–660–2688; www.alaskan.com/talkeetnadenali/). The Visitors Center can also help travelers book lodging in Talkeetna. There are numerous **bed and breakfasts** in the area. On a larger scale, the **Talkeetna Alaskan Lodge** (Talkeetna Spur Road; 888–959–9590; www.talkeetnalodge.com) offers more luxurious lodgings and spectacular views of Mount McKinley.

■ **DENALI NATIONAL PARK:** The centerpiece of the Denali National Park and Preserve is North America's highest mountain—20,320-foot Mount McKinley, also called Denali. But the park's more than six million acres also contain countless other spectacular mountains and many large glaciers. This protected land encompasses a complete subarctic ecosystem with large mammals such as grizzly bears, wolves, and moose. The park also accommodates a wide variety of activities including wildlife viewing, mountaineering, and backpacking. One of Denali's most popular excursions is an eleven-hour round trip to **Wonder Lake,** famous for its breathtaking views of Mount McKinley. Buses leave every half hour from the park entrance (800–622–7275).

■ Denali National Park was expanded in 1980 and now covers an area larger than the state of Massachusetts.

■ Talkeetna was founded as a railroad camp at the confluence of three rivers; its name means "river of plenty" in the language of the Tanaina Indians.

The **Denali Park Hotel,** located 1.5 miles inside the entrance, is the only lodging within the park; it also houses a restaurant and snack shop (800–276–7234; www.nps.gov/dena/). The park has seven **campgrounds** with a total of 291 sites. (For more information on camping, call 800–622–7275.) Many other **accommodations** are located within a short distance of the park. Most lodging is open only in summer. The most modern and luxurious nearby hotel is the **Denali Princess Lodge** located 1 mile from the entrance to the park (238.5 Mile Park Highway; 800–426–0500). It features panoramic views of the park and outdoor decks with hot tubs.

Alaska Railroad Engine #1 occupies a place of honor in front of the station in Anchorage.

■ **FAIRBANKS:** The end of the line for the AKRR, Alaska's second largest city is located in the heart of the interior, on the banks of the Chena River in the Tanana Valley. Summer visitors can expect twenty-one hours of daylight between mid-May and the beginning of August, while winter residents must tolerate less than four hours of daylight between mid-November and mid-January.

The **Fairbanks International Airport** (907–474–2500), 5 miles from downtown, is served by several major airlines. A number of bush carriers fly out of Fairbanks for more adventurous travelers wishing to explore Alaska's interior. **Fairbanks Convention and Visitors Bureau** (550 First Avenue; 907–456–5774; www.explorefairbanks.com) distributes a visitors guide and maps. The **Alaskaland** theme park (2400 Airport Way; 907–459–1087; www.fairbanks-alaska.com/alaskaland.htm) displays the restored railcar that brought President Warren G. Harding to Fairbanks to celebrate the completion of the Alaska Railroad in 1923. Alaskaland also features what it calls "a museum in progress," the ongoing renovation of Tanana Valley Railroad Engine #1. Built in 1899 for use in a coalmine, the engine is considered the oldest rail relic in Alaska. The running gear is all original and volunteers are reconstructing the cab and the boiler.

Two bed and breakfasts in Fairbanks are located near the Alaska Railroad Station: the **Fairbanks Exploration Inn** (505 Illinois Street; 888–452–1920; www.feinn.com) and the **All Seasons Inn** (763 Seventh Avenue; 888–451–6649; www.alaska.net/~inn).

OTHER DAY TRIPS

In addition to the Anchorage-Fairbanks route, the Alaska Railroad offers two other regularly scheduled trips. The "Coastal Classic" travels between Anchorage and the port city of Seward, a four-hour trip of spectacular scenery, as the train passes within a half-mile of three glaciers and travels over gorges and past several waterfalls. The "Glacier

Passengers may have to look closely to see Mount McKinley, which is often hidden in the clouds.

Discovery" is the railroad's newest route, running between Anchorage and the port community of Whittier in about two-and-a-half hours. While there's not much to do in Whittier, it is a good starting point for exploring Prince William Sound.

INFORMATION

- **Alaska Railroad Corporation**, P. O. Box 107500, Anchorage, AK 99510-7500; (907) 265–2494 or (800) 544–0552. **E-Mail:** reservations@akrr.com. **Web site:** www.alaskarailroad.com.
- **Denali National Park & Preserve**, P.O. Box 9, Denali Park, AK 99755; (907) 683–2294. **Web site:** www.nps.gov/dena/.
- **Anchorage:** www.anchorage.net
- **Fairbanks:** www.touralaska.org/fairbanks

The Adirondack

The two endpoints of Amtrak's Adirondack route are a study in contrast: the frenetic energy of New York and the refined European atmosphere of Montreal. Connecting them is a train ride filled with spectacular scenery. From the Hudson River Valley through New York's mountain regions to sweeping views of Lake Champlain, the Adirondack has earned its place as one of the most scenic train trips in the United States.

THE TRAIN
Amtrak's *Adirondack*

Amtrak is justifiably proud of its refurbished *Adirondack* line, which has been steadily upgraded over the past two decades. The train runs once a day, seven days a week, in both directions. Although the Sunday schedule runs a little later, Monday through Saturday the train leaves early in the morning with an early evening arrival.

■ If your primary interest is the Hudson River Valley, Amtrak's *Ethan Allen Express* follows the same route as the *Adirondack* between New York and Fort Edwards, and the trip takes less than four hours.

The *Adirondack*'s cars were redesigned to focus on the nostalgia and romance of rail travel. The exterior of the Heritage Coaches have been painted with a special *Adirondack* logo, and the interiors are gray, pink, and blue. The new cars also offer a smoother ride as well as fold-down trays, increased space for overhead luggage and legroom, and larger windows for viewing the scenery. Baggage cars have racks designed to carry fully assembled bicycles, skis, and snowboards for the convenience of weekend athletes.

The refurbishment resulted in the *Adirondack*'s receipt of the Odyssey Award for Cultural Heritage from the Travel Industry Association of America. Ridership continues to rise, making this one of Amtrak's most popular routes for leisure travelers.

THE ROUTE
New York City ~ Hudson River Valley ~ Adirondack Mountains ~ Lake Champlain ~ Montreal

The straight 400-mile trip between New York City and Montreal takes ten hours and can be a relaxing, enjoyable train experience by itself, although many visitors choose to take one or more day trips along the way. The *Adirondack* makes more than a dozen stops with plenty of lodging and transportation options available at just about every stop.

The tracks parallel the Hudson River for about 100 miles, providing particularly scenic views, first of the wooded Palisades on the New Jersey shoreline, then of the richly historic Hudson River Valley. One of the first stops is Croton-Harmon, the place to debark for explorations of the region's many historic mansions open to the public.

North of Albany, the route climbs into the surprisingly rugged northern New York State countryside, passing near or through many famous resorts, such as Saratoga Springs, playground of the summer horse-racing set. Here in the foothills of the Adirondack Mountains, the tracks cross back to the east side of the Hudson.

As the train travels into the Champlain Valley, it traces the eastern border of **Adirondack Park,** a six-million-acre patchwork of public and private lands. Best known for its mountains and lakes, this region is a place of uncommon serenity and beauty. The train glides past bucolic farms and forested areas accessible only by rail. **Lake Champlain** offers spectacular views and recreational boating, fishing, and camping during the summer months.

After parting company with Lake Champlain, the train heads through forests

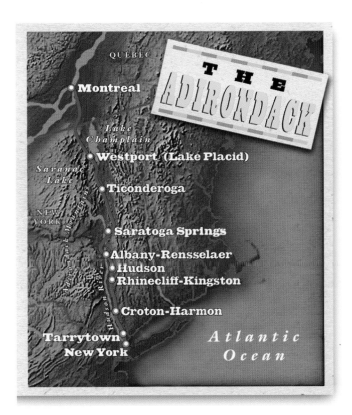

The following text appears on the map:

QUEBEC

• **Montreal**

Lake Champlain

• **Westport (Lake Placid)**

Saranac Lake

• **Ticonderoga**

NEW YORK

• **Saratoga Springs**

• **Albany-Rensselaer**
• **Hudson**
• **Rhinecliff-Kingston**

• **Croton-Harmon**

Tarrytown •
New York

Atlantic Ocean

■ The Adirondacks were named by a surveyor who thought it the name of an Indian tribe that once hunted there. Actually the word is an Iroquois term of derision meaning "bark eaters."

and cornfields to Rouses Point, the last stop in the United States and the customs check for southbound passengers on the *Adirondack* line. The route crosses the border at Cantic, Quebec, where northbound passengers are checked by Canadian customs. The stop is usually very brief, though it is necessary to have proof of citizenship. The train then travels through the agricultural Richelieu River Valley before crossing the St. Lawrence River into Montreal.

RATES

Based on a round-trip ticket, fares are $52 between New York and Montreal if you're traveling on a weekday. On weekends the one-way fare rises to $57. Amtrak offers special packages during the fall foliage and skiing seasons; these include train fare and hotel accommodations at some destinations. Check with a ticket agent for more information.

■ The boundaries of Adirondack Park are commonly known as "the blue line," because the first map outlining the park a century ago highlighted the area in blue.

■ To reach one of Adirondack Park's most popular destinations—**Blue Mountain Lake**—visitors from New York once had to take an overnight train to Utica, transfer to a steamboat, change to the world's shortest standard-gauge railroad (less than a mile long), and make a final transfer to another steamboat.

With Amtrak's New York Unlimited fare, passengers can make unrestricted stopovers to any destination along the *Adirondack* route. Reservations are required, and some blackout dates may apply, so passengers should check with Amtrak.

WHAT'S INCLUDED: The *Adirondack* offers only coach seating, and all onboard food or amenities are in addition to the rail fare.

CUSTOMS

Amtrak passengers traveling into Canada are required to go through customs. Although time is allotted in the schedule for these inspections, there are occasional delays. Passengers entering Canada are required to have a passport, birth certificate, citizenship certificate, or naturalization certificate. A driver's license is *not* sufficient.

ON BOARD

DINING: The *Adirondack* features three refurbished cafe-lounge cars with names that reflect the route—"L'Auberge Laurentian," "Saratoga Inn," and "Adirondack Lodge." The food is more varied than what you might expect from Amtrak, which is clearly trying to cater to the train's international travelers. The menu is written in English and French and includes foods and beverages native to the region.

DRESS CODE: Those heading to the Adirondacks for outdoor winter activities or north to Montreal should be prepared for cold temperatures. Keep in mind that winters in Montreal can be so harsh that town planners constructed an extensive underground city!

PASSENGERS: Although some people use the *Adirondack* for regular commutes into New York, weekend trippers and other vacationers are more common. For that reason, the atmosphere on board is more congenial than on shorter Amtrak runs that cater to a business crowd.

CREW: Customer service received particular attention in the overhaul of the *Adirondack* line. All ticket agents and crew members now undergo a specialized customer-service training program. The effort has apparently paid off—the crew is friendly and helpful.

Mirror Lake is one of the almost 3,000 lakes and ponds that add to the uncommon beauty of the Adirondack Mountains.

MAJOR STOPS

Passengers planning excursions along the *Adirondack*'s route can easily coordinate entertaining side trips with the train's schedule. It is possible to get off at one stop, rent a car for a day or two, and rejoin the train at another stop farther north or simply pick the train up at the same station. You'll need to make travel arrangements once you're off the train, but Amtrak's web site and booking agents have information about lodging and transportation services available from its stations.

■ **NEW YORK CITY:** For now, Amtrak travelers in New York City have to make do with the current **Pennsylvania Station** (212–582–6875), which for thirty years has been located at Seventh Avenue and West 32nd Street underneath **Madison Square Garden**. This congested space is shared by two commuter railroads and half-a-million daily travelers. All of that will change when the station moves to the historic **James A. Farley Post Office Building** across the street. The new station will attempt to re-create the majesty of the original Penn Station, which was torn down in 1963. For a hotel with a historic flair, try the landmark **Hotel Pennsylvania** (the inspiration

HIGHLIGHT

■ *Well aware of the treasures that surrounded the family's treasured Kykuit estate, John D. Rockefeller, Jr., founded Sleepy Hollow Restorations in 1951 to preserve the history and culture of the Hudson River Valley. Now known as Historic Hudson Valley, the organization operates six architectural masterpieces as living history museums: Kykuit; Montgomery Place, a Federal-style mansion; Philipsburg Manor, a working 18th-century farm; Sunnyside, Washington Irving's historic home; Union Church of Pocantico Hills, featuring stained glass windows by Henri Matisse and Marc Chagall; and Van Cortlandt Manor, which contains an exceptional collection of decorative arts. Historic Hudson Valley: 150 White Plains Road, Tarrytown, NY 10591; (914) 631–8200; www.hudsonvalley.org.*

for Glenn Miller's "Pennsylvania-6-5000") located at 401 Seventh Avenue (212–736–5000) just across from the Station.

■ Until a survey in 1837 showed that the Adirondacks' Mount Marcy was more than a mile high, the better-known Catskills were thought to be New York's highest mountains.

First time visitors to the Big Apple can pick up maps, brochures, and other tourist essentials at the **Times Square Visitors Center** at 1560 Broadway near 47th Street (212–768–1560). Certainly worth a stop is **Grand Central Terminal** (42nd Street between Park and Lexington Avenues; 212–340–2583; www.grandcentralterminal.com). See the spectacular results of a recent twelve-year renovation, in which years of grime and dirt were removed from the main concourse of this Beaux-Arts beauty. The terminal's interior space was redesigned and expanded and now bustles with new shops and restaurants.

■ **RHINECLIFF:** A stopover at Rhinecliff provides easy access to a pleasant stay in the quaint nearby village of Rhinebeck. Small shops and galleries line the streets of this picturesque town, which is also the jumping-off point for a visit to the **Franklin D. Roosevelt National Historic Site** (914–229–8114; www.nps.gov/hofr), FDR's lifelong home and the site of the nation's first presidential library.

■ The first rail lines in the Adirondacks were built to haul timber out, but operators quickly realized that they could also make a profit by bringing tourists in.

Nearby, the stunning fifty-room **Vanderbilt Mansion** (511 Albany Post Road, Hyde Park, NY 12538; 914–229–9115; www.nps.gov/vama) features original decor and furnishings, as well as extensive gardens. Hyde Park is also home to some of the best cooking in the country, thanks to the **Culinary Institute of America** (433 Albany Post Road; 914–471–6608; www.ciachef.edu), which has five public restaurants, each featuring the cuisine of a different region of the world.

Ten small buildings in the center of Rhinebeck make up the **Beekman Arms** (4 Mill Street; 914–876–7077; www.beekmanarms.com), America's oldest continuously operated inn, which provides comfortable lodging in Colonial or Victorian style. A short distance out of town is the **Olde Rhinebeck Inn** (37 Wurtemburg Road; 914–871–1745; www.rhinebeckinn.com), an early-American farmhouse listed on the National Register of Historic Places.

■ **SARATOGA SPRINGS:** The writer John Reed said that it was "society, sports, and sin" that made Saratoga Springs America's premier resort of the 19th century. People originally came to "take the waters" that bubbled from the springs and were said to have curative powers. Visitors can taste those very same waters in Congress Park, where the town's **information center** is located (297 Broadway; 518–587–3241). For six weeks every summer, the most elite horses in the world come to race in Saratoga's gabled grandstand.

The **National Museum of Racing** (191 Union Avenue; 518–584–0400) is across the street. Saratoga is also a showplace of American architecture, especially Greek Revival, Gothic Revival, and Queen Anne. The city boasts 900 buildings listed on the National Register of Historic Places.

For opulent surroundings, the **Adelphi Hotel** (365 Broadway; 518–587–4688; www.adelphihotel.com) is Saratoga's showplace hotel. For information on **bed-and-breakfast** accommodations in Saratoga Springs or anywhere in the Adirondacks, a good place to start is the **Adirondacks B&B Association** (P.O. Box 801, Lake George, NY 12845; www.adirondackbb.com).

■ **TICONDEROGA:** The famous star-shaped **Fort Ticonderoga** (Route 74, about a mile west of the train station; 518–585–2821; www.ticonderoga.org) was in British hands when Ethan Allen and his Green Mountain Boys, together with Colonel Benedict Arnold, took it in a surprise attack in 1775. Today the fort is restored according to early plans and includes a museum with a collection of weapons, paintings, and uniforms. During the summer a fife and drum corps conducts demonstrations and drills on the parade grounds.

There are several **chain motels** in the Ticonderoga area, or for a cozier environment, Westport offers several B&Bs.

■ **WESTPORT/LAKE PLACID:** The hamlet of Lake Placid lies not far from the *Adirondack's* Westport stop. (During the winter, Amtrak arranges for motor-coach connections between Westport and Lake Placid.) Site of the 1932 and 1980 Winter Olympics, Lake Placid offers a variety of activities in the summer and winter. Tours of various parts of the **Olympic Complex** are available. Adventurous visitors can ride a chairlift to the top of the ski-jumping tower (518–946–2223) or even take a run down the only dedicated bobsled run in the United States, with professional drivers and brakemen powering a bobsled on wheels (518–523–4436). **The New York Olympic Regional Development Authority** now manages the facilities and its year-round activities (518–523–1655; www.orda.org). For information on activities in the area, contact the **Lake Placid Convention and**

Although the tallest peaks are concentrated in 1,200 square miles of the Adirondacks' east-central region, the range actually encompasses 11,000 square miles, almost one-fourth of the state of New York.

Visitors Bureau (800–44PLACID; www.lakeplacid.com).

There are several resorts and hotels in the area, as well as numerous **bed and breakfasts.** Among the more atmospheric lodgings are the **Lake Placid Lodge,** a small but luxurious hotel outfitted in Adirondack style (Whiteface Inn Road; 518–523–2700), and the **Adirondack Inn by the Lake** (217 Main Street; 518–523–2424; www.lakeplacid.com/adkinn).

■ **MONTREAL:** Montreal's main train station, the **Gare Centrale,** is located downtown at 2 Place Ville Marie, minutes away from historic **Old Montreal** and the **Golden Square Mile** of elegant 19th-century homes. From the station you can also access Montreal's famous **Underground City**. Hiding beneath the city's busy streets are numerous hotels, offices, movie theaters, shops, restaurants, a skating rink, even entire museums, universities, and the home ice of the Montreal Canadiens. One of the city's historic hotels, **The Queen Elizabeth** (or le Reine Elizabeth, as it's known in Montreal) rises directly over the train station (900 René Lévesque Boulevard West; 800–441–1414).

INFORMATION

- ■ **Amtrak:** 30th Street Station, 30th and Market Streets, Philadelphia, PA 19104; (800) USA–RAIL. **E-Mail:** service@sales.amtrak.com. **Web site:** www.amtrak.com
- ■ **New York City:** www.nycvisit.com or www.nyctourist.com
- ■ **Hudson Valley:** www.hudsonriver.com
- ■ **Rhinebeck:** www.rhinebeck.com
- ■ **Saratoga Springs:** www.saratoga.org
- ■ **Adirondacks:** www.Adirondacks.org
- ■ **Lake Placid:** www.lakeplacid.com
- ■ **Fort Ticonderoga:** www.fort-ticonderoga.org
- ■ **Montreal:** www.tourism-montreal.org

Mexico's Copper Canyon

Recently voted the world's most exciting train ride, the trip through Mexico's Copper Canyon brings both unparalleled scenery and a chance to experience the native culture of the secluded Tarahumara Indians. Passengers take the Sierra Madre Express *into places only a train can go, back to a time when wilderness was really wild.*

THE TRAIN
Sierra Madre Express

There is no question that this trip is about adventure and experiencing rugged wilderness. The *Sierra Madre Express* provides a unique trip on vintage railcars to one of the most remote areas of Mexico. Considered the flagship private rail carrier to Northern Mexico, the *Sierra Madre Express* is made up of lovingly restored railcars from the 1940s and the 1950s. The diner and observation-lounge sleepers are carried on all runs with additional sleeping and lounge cars as bookings require. The "Divisadero" car features an outdoor deck. The "Arizona," an observation-lounge car built in 1946 by the Pullman Company, is highlighted by its glass-enclosed observation area and a full bar. The "Chile Verde," also built in 1946, contains an informal dining area. The domed "Tucson" offers a comfortable lounge as well as a raised observation dome, which serves as the formal dining area. All food, water, and ice are brought on board from the United States.

■ Photographers and bird-watchers get a special treat on this train, which features an open-air lounge and observation area.

Part of the appeal of the *Sierra Madre Express* is its homespun character. The train was the brainchild of Peter Robbins, who purchased his first vintage car to live in. The interior design of the cars is casually comfortable, adding to the trip's relaxed atmosphere.

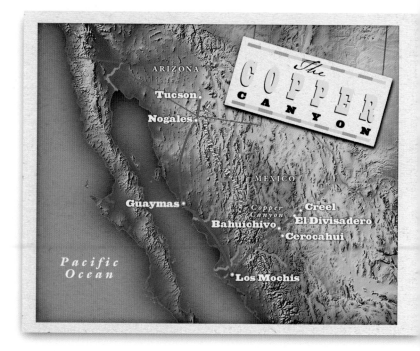

THE ROUTE
Tucson ~ Divisadero ~ Creel ~ Cerocahui ~ Sonoran Desert ~ Tucson

Deeper than the Grand Canyon and four times larger, Copper Canyon is readily accessible only by means of a rail line through country so rugged it took fifty years to lay the tracks. Over the course of a week, the *Sierra Madre Express* travels more than 1,300 miles over elevations that range from sea level to 8,000 feet. The route traverses more than a hundred tunnels and bridges, many so high they are not for the faint of heart.

■ Although there is a specific Copper Canyon near the village of Tejaban, the name is used to describe the total canyon system.

The trip begins and ends in Tucson, Arizona, where, on the first day, passengers attend a welcoming dinner and spend the night at a luxury hotel. A motor-coach tour the next morning through Tucson and the Santa Cruz Valley arrives in Nogales, Mexico, in mid-afternoon. Passengers are welcomed aboard with a cocktail reception and full dinner, then spend the night exploring the train and settling in. The train crosses the Sonoran Desert and skirts the Sea of Cortez during the night.

The next morning the train climbs steadily through the foothills of the Sierra Madre Mountains. At the heart of the Copper Canyon experience is the famed Chihuahua al Pacifico Railway that runs between Los Mochis and Chihuahua. The 400 miles of this rail line are considered an engineering miracle, as the train rises through some of Mexico's most majestic but forbidding mountain country. Arriving at Divisadero in mid-afternoon, passengers have time to enjoy mountain paths that provide breathtaking views from the canyon's rim. The trip uses the wonderful Posada Barrancas Mirador Hotel as a home base for day trips to other parts of the canyon.

■ Except for the Arctic zone, the *Sierra Madre Express* travels through each of the earth's climate zones, from subtropics in the canyon bottoms to conifer forests at 8,000 feet, making for a wide diversity of flora and fauna.

■ Copper Canyon evokes forbidding images from the classic 1948 movie *The Treasure of the Sierra Madre*. That tale of three ill-matched gold prospectors was shot almost entirely on location.

The next day's outing to Creel, in the heart of Tarahumara country, finds the train negotiating a figure-eight loop, one of the few places in the world where a route's tracks actually cross over themselves. After a tour of an old Tarahumara cave, lunch is served on the train and visitors have the afternoon for shopping or exploring the town. The next morning is free for hiking, shopping, or even taking a horseback tour of the canyons. After lunch, the train departs on a two-hour ride to Bahuichivo, and then a forty-five-minute ride on local buses leads to the Hotel El Mision in the 17th-century mission village of Cerocahui. This is where the trip gets

HIGHLIGHT

■ *The name "Copper Canyon" actually refers to a series of more than twenty interconnected canyons in the heart of the Sierra Madre. These canyons were carved by a series of rivers from volcanic rock, 1,000 to 1,500 feet thick, which was laid down around 30 million years ago. The canyons cover a vast area almost four times larger and 280 feet deeper than Arizona's Grand Canyon. Known locally as the* Barranca del Cobre, *the canyons carve incisions into the igneous heart of the continent so deep that they host their own unique ecosystems.*

■ At one point in its journey, the train makes a 180-degree turn inside a mountain, emerging in the opposite direction and still climbing. This location is where the Chihuahua al Pacifico railroad was dedicated in 1961.

■ The American Society of Travel Writers voted the *Sierra Madre Express* trip through Copper Canyon "the world's most exciting train ride" in 1998.

rugged. The roads are steep and rutted, so the ride is bumpy and dusty, and while the hotel is comfortable, electricity in Cerocahui is limited to a few hours in the evening. The hotel's generator also operates for about an hour in the morning, and the rooms have kerosene lamps and woodstove heaters. Guests have the option of spending the next morning exploring Cerocahui or taking a bus tour to **Gallego Outlook.** Although the four-hour trip can be rough and dusty, the latter provides an unforgettable view of the canyons. After a lunch back at the hotel, passengers board the train again for the descent toward the coast and a farewell dinner served on board. The following morning, passengers enjoy daylight views of the Sonoran Desert, covered in darkness a week ago. A night at the Tucson hotel, breakfast the next morning, and airport transfers are included. Although the *Sierra Madre Express* arranges some of its own annual trips, the majority are handled by Tauck Tours (see p. 31), whose itineraries differ slightly.

ACCOMMODATIONS

The train's five refurbished passenger cars offer a variety of sleeping accommodations. Sleepers offer the standard bunk configuration but also include rooms with two lower twins. Sleepers are small but comfortable, and each double room has a sink and toilet; single compartments share a toilet. Although there are no onboard showers, the tour calls for only two of the seven nights to be spent on the train.

RATES

Per person; $2,740 single occupancy with shared toilet; $2,545 double bedroom with private toilet; $2,745 double in the Drawing Room of the "Arizona" car. *Note:* Prices will increase by $125 in 2001.

WHAT'S INCLUDED: All meals (except two dinners in Tucson), sight-seeing, transportation round-trip between the train and Tucson, lodging, drinks on board the train, guides and commentary by the train staff, luggage handling, tipping, and transfers.

WHAT'S NOT INCLUDED: Extra drinks at hotel overnights (cocktail parties are included at most hotels), horseback rides, helicopter tours, and souvenirs.

CUSTOMS

To enter Mexico, passengers must provide proof of citizenship, preferably a passport, or a birth certificate and a photo ID. No immunizations are required.

The Posada Barrancas Mirador Hotel clings to the rim of the canyon, offering spectacular views.

The Sierra Madre Express *navigates the famed Chihuahua al Pacifico Railway.*

ON BOARD

DINING: American and Mexican-style food is available through-out the trip, and although the food is good, selection in the Mexican hotels is often limited to two or three entrees. American bottled water is provided on the train and in the hotels.

DRESS CODE: During the rail portion of the trip, the railroad recommends jeans and casual clothes, stressing "the *Sierra Madre* is not a black-tie express!"

PASSENGERS: *Sierra Madre Express* makes clear that this is not a trip for everybody. Passengers must be in good health and surefoot-ed, as much of the sight-seeing involves walking on uneven paths. In addition, the tour spends three-and-a-half days at elevations reaching 8,000 feet and temperatures can vary widely. The railroad says the ideal person is well traveled, enjoys discovering unique destinations, and is willing to accept the unexpected and local ways.

CREW: The *Sierra Madre Express* is operated by American crews who work alongside the Mexican workers who run the locomotives. A crew of six and an experienced bilingual guide accompany each tour.

HIGHLIGHT

■ *A trip into Copper Canyon provides not only dramatic scenery but also a glimpse into the life and culture of the Tarahumara Indians, considered to be the North American tribe most isolated from modern civilization. Known for their fine basket making and traditional cave dwellings, the Tarahumara live a primitive life, subsisting mostly on corn, beans, and livestock, with many migrating seasonally to take advantage of longer growing seasons. Up to 50,000 Tarahumara live in the wilderness of Copper Canyon, most in small family groups. In the winter they live in caves, moving into small log cabins in the summer.*

MAJOR STOPS

■ **TUCSON:** Founded by the Spanish in 1775, Tucson is built on the site of a much older Indian village and has been home to villages and farms for at least 2,000 years. With its unique blend of Indian, Spanish, Mexican, and Anglo heritages, Tucson retains the charm of its desert frontier roots. The current Tucson **train station** is located at 400 East Toole Avenue (520–623–4442) in the downtown area. Construction is underway on a new transportation center in the former Southern Pacific passenger depot. **Tucson International Airport** (520–573–8000) is about 10 miles south of downtown. There is much to see in Tucson for visitors who want to explore the city before or after their trip to Copper Canyon.

■ Travelers through Copper Canyon are often amazed at the number of different birds they see. The region boasts at least 270 species, many of which cannot be found in the United States.

The **Arizona-Sonora Desert Museum** (2021 North Kinney Road; 520–883–1380; www.desertmuseum.org) is one of the area's top attractions. Located in Saguaro National Park, the museum is actually a zoo, natural history museum, and botanical garden rolled into one. Visitors can roam freely among outstanding natural habitat exhibits of Sonoran Desert animals, plants, and ecology. The **Arizona Historical Society,** on the campus of the University of Arizona (949 East Second Street; 520–628–5774), highlights exhibits recounting

Arizona's colorful cultural history from Spanish colonial times through the present.

■ **DIVISADERO:** At an elevation of about 8,000 feet, Divisadero provides terrific views of Copper Canyon. The stop also introduces guests to the culture of the Tarahumara Indians. The tracks are lined with colorfully dressed Tarahumara women who have come to sell their handcrafted baskets woven from native grasses and pine needles. Many of the basket makers hike long distances from the depths of the canyon every day to sell their work. Women and children can also be found at the train station making gorditas and burritos on steel drum stoves.

■ Running up and down the steep canyons is an important part of the Tarahumara culture. A means of both transportation and communication in this rugged area, it is also a sport in which villages compete against each other.

■ The baskets of the Tarahumara are made out of agave leaves and pine needles. The Indians are also known for their carved wooden dolls dressed in traditional clothing.

The **Posada Barrancas Mirador** reflects the local culture. Literally perched on the rim of the canyon, the hotel was built by nearby Tarahumara Indians, and everything from the ornaments and the tile to the adobe walls is handmade. Native Tarahumara people are often on hand to entertain guests with traditional dances and games. The hotel offers gracious service and deluxe rooms, each with a view of the canyon. The food is good, and the hotel has twenty-four-hour electricity, with room heat supplied by electric stoves. If nighttime observers can take their eyes off the spectacular display of stars above, distant Indian campfires can often be seen from the canyon walls.

■ **CREEL:** The town of Creel is the heart of Tarahumara country. Now predominantly a lumber and tourism town, Creel was founded in 1906 by former Governor Enrique Creel. Just south of Creel is **Cusarare,** site of an 18th-century mission in the native Tarahumara style. A little farther away a hiking trail leads to the cascades of **Cusarare Falls.**

■ **CEROCAHUI:** Known as the most beautiful village in the canyon, Cerocahui is a rustic town of a few houses and hotels built around an old mission church. The town was founded in 1680 by an Italian Jesuit, and its 300-year-old sandstone church, with lovely stained-glass windows, was extensively reconstructed during the 1940s. The Jesuits still operate a boarding school here for native Tarahumara children. The town's 600 residents are an eclectic mix of loggers, Indians, cowboys, and westerners serving the tourist industry.

Once a grand hacienda, the **Hotel El Mision** has been converted into a rustic lodge with colorful Indian and colonial decor. Here visitors encounter the realities of living in isolation. Electricity is limited to a few hours each evening; the hotel relies on a generator to provide an hour of electricity in the morning. Rooms are equipped with woodstove heaters and kerosene lamps. For adventurous travelers the hotel can arrange a horseback excursion to scenic sites in the area, including beautiful **Wicochi Falls.**

INFORMATION

■ **Sierra Madre Express:** P.O. Box 26381, Tucson, AZ 85726–6381; (800) 666–0346 or (520) 747–0346. **E-mail:** adventure@sierramadreexpress.com. **Web site:** www.sierramadreexpress.com.
■ **Tauck Tours:** 276 Post Road West, Westport, CT 06880; (203) 226–0911. **E-mail:** info@tauck.com.
■ **Tucson Online:** www.pima.com
■ **Arizona Tourism:** www.arizonaguide.com

The Chihuahua al Pacifico Railway is an engineering marvel, built through some of the most rugged terrain in North America.

The Rockies by Rail

It's hard to know what is more spectacular: the grandeur of the passing scenery or the experience on board America's premier luxury train. The American Orient Express *carries you through the towering glory of the Rocky Mountains and a series of dramatic canyons to the striking splendor of Wyoming's national parks.*

THE TRAIN
American Orient Express

Traveling on board the *American Orient Express* whisks you back in time to the golden age of extravagant streamliners. Surrounded by elegance, passengers experience a once-in-a-lifetime "land cruise" across the Rocky Mountains. Although the *AOE* itineraries change regularly, the journey's ports of call are only part of the pleasure. For many, the train itself is the true destination.

■ The Continental Divide marks the Rockies' highest point. On one side rivers flow west to the Pacific Ocean; on the other side the water begins the long journey east to the Atlantic.

The train is made up of fifteen exquisite railcars, dating from the 1940s and 1950s, gathered from museums and private collections throughout America. In 1988 the cars underwent extensive refurbishing, at a cost of about one million dollars each. Sporting the royal blue and gold colored exteriors of the deluxe trains of Europe, the carriages pay homage to the romantic age of rail travel. Each car's interior has been painstakingly detailed, surrounding passengers in warm mahogany, sumptuous leather, polished brass, and period artwork. In addition to its five Pullman sleeping cars, the train includes two luxurious club cars (each outfitted with a baby grand piano). The club and observation cars each offer plush seating for thirty people, and they display distinct decor.

The sleepers have been updated with modern comforts such as air-conditioning and private lavatories. Each carriage has a private attendant to facilitate easy scheduling of the shared shower, even providing a fluffy robe and towels.

THE ROUTE
Denver ~ Colorado National Monument ~ Arches National Park ~ Salt Lake City ~ Grand Teton National Park ~ Yellowstone National Park

The seven-day, six-night Rockies and Yellowstone journey begins in Denver, where passengers sleep overnight on board the train. The staff helps you settle in with a welcoming reception, ensuring you're relaxed, rested, and ready to roll in the morning. The scenic highlight of this 1,019-mile–long trip may well be the first full day of travel between Denver and Salt Lake City. As the train climbs through the heart of Colorado's Rocky Mountains, passengers feast their eyes on dramatic mountain and canyon vistas, views that cannot be seen by car. Following the historic tracks of the Denver and Rio Grande Western Railroad, the train snakes through rock tunnels and steep gorges, then turns to follow the mighty Colorado River, whose path the tracks parallel for 240 miles.

■ The train speeds through the 6.2-mile Moffat Tunnel in just nine minutes, a journey across the Continental Divide that once took five hours, even in perfect weather.

At Grand Junction, Colorado, the journey pauses for a land tour of the mosaic of domes, canyons, and plateaus carved over millions of years and now designated the Colorado National Monument. Later

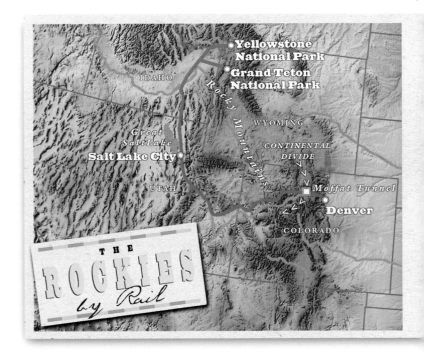

there is another stop for Arches National Park, the world's largest concentration of natural sandstone arches. The next day finds the mountains yielding to Utah's earth-toned landscapes as the train heads for the state's capital, Salt Lake City. The following day is spent exploring this western town, with tours of the Mormon Temple, the Tabernacle gardens and monuments, and the striking Beehive House, which served as Brigham Young's governor's mansion.

Once underway, the train continues north to Idaho Falls, where motor coaches make the hour-and-a-half journey into Grand Teton National Park. An estimated 10,000 elk still roam the high country, along with countless moose and black bears.

During most of its trips, the *American Orient Express* lodges passengers for two nights at the Jackson Lake Lodge, the centerpiece of the Grand Teton park. After the first night at the lodge, passengers have a free morning at Grand Teton National Park to enjoy a boat cruise, horseback riding, hiking, or a round of golf. Motor coaches

---

The plush seating and bay window of the "New York" observation car are characteristic of the luxury on board the American Orient Express.

■ If the *American Orient Express* is too rich for your blood, consider Amtrak's *California Zephyr,* which follows the same route between Denver and Salt Lake City.

then make the short trip to Yellowstone National Park, allowing a day and a half to explore its amazing beauty. With more than two million acres of protected land, Yellowstone is known for its numerous boiling springs, mud pots, and geysers, which are churned by the convergence of water and molten rock miles below the surface. Ninety-nine percent of the park's land remains undeveloped, providing a wide range of habitats for large and varied wildlife populations.

After a full day at Yellowstone, passengers return to the waiting train for a relaxing farewell dinner. The *AOE* then journeys back to Salt Lake City, the end-point of the trip. This tour also operates in reverse, with four departures available in each direction: one each in June, September, October, and November.

ACCOMMODATIONS

Passengers on the *American Orient Express* can choose from several overnight carriage options. Standard compartments, here called **Vintage Pullman,** have an upper and lower berth and a full-size couch. A **Single Sleeper** provides a lower berth and a single sofa seat. The larger **Parlor Suite** offers two lower berths, a full couch, and a single sofa seat; an extra upper berth can fold down should there be a third passenger. For the ultimate in luxury, the **Presidential Suite** is a double-size cabin with two lower berths, two single sofa seats, and its own shower.

RATES

Six nights aboard the *American Orient Express,* per person, based on double occupancy: Vintage Pullman: $2,990; Single Sleeper: $3,790; Parlor Suite: $4,390; Presidential Suite: $4,990. This is understandably a popular trip. *AOE* recommends you reserve six months or more in advance. Small discounts are provided for early birds.

WHAT'S INCLUDED: All nights aboard the *American Orient Express* and hotel accommodations; welcome and farewell receptions; all meals; soft drinks, bottled water, and house wine with dinner; all excursions and other group activities; lectures and presentations; baggage handling; gratuities to guides, escorts, and drivers; complimentary toiletries package.

HIGHLIGHT

■ For many travelers on board the American Orient Express, *the highlight of the train itself is the very last car: the "New York" observation car. The historic rounded car features a plush circular settee; deep, large windows; and fine mahogany woodwork. Its centerpiece is a dramatic horseshoe-shaped bar. A veteran of the famous* 20th Century Limited, *the "New York" observation car was dedicated in 1948 by U.S. President Dwight D. Eisenhower and comedian Beatrice Lillie. The car was one of New York Central's classic Creek series of observation cars and ran the rails of the* 20th Century Limited *between New York and Chicago for 20 years.*

WHAT'S NOT INCLUDED: Airfare and taxes, and other transportation to and from the train; accident, baggage, and/or cancellation insurance; airport transfers; personal expenses such as laundry, telephone, fax charges, or taxis; liquor; traditional gratuities to train staff. A $500 deposit is required on booking, half of which is refundable until sixty days prior to departure. Because no refunds are allowed in the sixty-day period before the trip, *AOE* highly recommends trip insurance coverage.

ON BOARD

DINING: Dine in style in the dining cars on tables set with china, crystal, and linen. The two dining cars—the "Chicago" and the "Zurich"—are decorated with rich inlaid paneling and tables set for two or four. There's plenty of open seating and leisurely dinner hours give you time to relax and enjoy the scenery while choosing from five entree selections prepared by accomplished chefs. Relying heavily on fresh local ingredients obtained at stops along the way, the chefs are known for creating regional specialties such as Copper River salmon or seared venison, with appetizers that include wild mushroom puff pastry and Anjou pear torte with créme fraîche for dessert. On the Rockies and Yellowstone route, selections reflect the area's Basque settlers and reliance on game

and beef. Many dishes follow recipes from train chefs of the past. And despite the challenges of space and limited availability of ingredients, *AOE* is able to meet the special dietary needs of passengers, including vegetarian and kosher meals. An onboard sommelier offers wines from California, Washington State, and France.

In the morning, a continental breakfast is offered in the club cars while a full menu awaits the hungry in the dining cars. A porter will also deliver coffee and juice to your compartment. If the midday meal falls during an off-board touring time, the chefs either prepare a box lunch or the tour stops at a local restaurant, usually one featuring regional cuisine. Once passengers are back on board, afternoon tea with pastries is available in the club cars.

DRESS CODE: Despite its elegance, the *American Orient Express* does not require dresses or jackets in the evening or at dinner. Dress is smart casual, with jackets and ties optional.

PASSENGERS: The *AOE* tries to foster a congenial, club-like atmosphere among its 108 passengers. Although some older children travel with parents or grandparents, the tenor of the trip is not suitable for young children. Because this trip includes moderately strenuous activities such as hiking and stair climbing, *AOE* expects passengers to be in good health and to enjoy traveling as part of a group.

CREW: The train staff includes expert guides and lecturers who offer commentary on a variety of historical, cultural, and scientific subjects, both

Luxurious dining amid outstanding scenery is part of the pleasure of traveling on the American Orient Express.

on the train and during the side excursions. A pianist provides music during the cocktail hour.

MAJOR STOPS

■ **DENVER:** Union Station in downtown Denver is at Seventeenth Street at Wynkoop Street, with **Denver International Airport** (303–342–2000), 25 miles west on I-70. Express bus service is available from the airport to downtown. While Denver's soaring skyscrapers speak to the mile-high city's prospering present, much of the city still reflects its western past. Areas like the historic district of **Lower Downtown** (**LoDo** to locals) feature restaurants, art galleries, and nightclubs housed in century-old buildings. A mile-long pedestrian mall cutting through the heart of downtown is surrounded by a series of parks and plazas. Nearby are some of the city's top attractions, including the **U.S. Mint** (West Colfax Avenue and Cherokee Street; 303–844–3584), the **Denver Art Museum** (100 West Fourteenth Avenue; 303–640–2793; www.denverartmuseum.org),

■ The train was once the only way to get to Yellowstone. Visitors were left at the north entrance and often spent up to ten days going around the park.

■ Old Faithful is not actually the largest geyser at Yellowstone. It has become so popular because it erupts so frequently, an average of 20 times a day.

and the **Colorado History Museum** (1300 Broadway; 303–866–3682). Train buffs should consider leaving extra time before the journey begins to visit the **Colorado Railroad Museum** (17155 West Forty-fourth Avenue; 800–365–6263 or 303–279–4591; www.crrm.org), 12 miles west of Denver in Golden, Colorado. Display tracks, complete with rare three-way stub switches and century-old switch stands, hold many historic narrow- and standard-gauge locomotives and cars. The museum building houses the largest known collection of historic records, mementos, arti-facts, and pictures of Colorado railroads.

The ultimate downtown hotel in Denver is the **Brown Palace** at 321 Seventeenth Street (303–297–3111; www.brownpalace.com). Rooms are decorated in high Victorian style and the luxurious atrium lobby is capped by a stained-glass ceiling nine stories up. The **Bed and Breakfast Innkeepers of Colorado** can direct visitors to cozier accommodations (P.O. Box 38416, Depart-ment S–95, Colorado Springs, CO 80937; 800–265–7696).

■ **COLORADO NATIONAL MONUMENT:** This national park offers a stunning variety of geologic features, from towering red sandstone monoliths to deep, sheer-walled canyons. Wildlife, including desert bighorn and coyotes, is abundant.

■ **ARCHES NATIONAL PARK:** The scenery is quite different at Arches National Park, which features the greatest number of natural sandstone arches in the world. The arches began to form 300 million years ago, when salt water from a nearby ocean flooded the area.

■ **GRAND TETON NATIONAL PARK:** Although Yellowstone to the north gets more attention, the Grand Teton National Park presents striking scenery of its own, with its rugged, gray-granite mountains offering an enduring wildlife habitat. Here, jagged vertical peaks of the Teton Range rise precipitously, as high as 7,000 feet above the Snake River plain. One favorite scenic spot is **Jenny Lake,** a natural reflecting pool for the mountains above. Grand Teton National Park was established in 1929 and grew to its present size with the addition of Rockefeller family land donated in the 1940s. Trained guides accompany the **park tours,** offering details about history, geology, and wildlife. Typically, passengers stay amid

the rustic beauty of the park's **Jackson
Lake Lodge**. Situated on a bluff with
spectacular views across the water of
Jackson Lake to the skyline of the
Tetons, the lodge offers guest cottage
rooms located on either side of the rustic timber and stone main lodge.

■ **YELLOWSTONE
NATIONAL PARK:** The
grandmother of all national parks,
Yellowstone offers spectacular wildlife
viewing, water displays, and dense
forests. Though it can be crowded with
tourists at times, wildlife such as black
and grizzly bears, bald eagles, and
herds of mule deer roam through the
two million acres of protected land.
The more than 10,000 boiling springs,
mud pots, and geysers—including **Old
Faithful**—attest to the geothermal
activity miles below the earth's surface.

■ **SALT LAKE CITY:** The **Rio
Grande Depot** (801–532–3472) is
located in downtown Salt Lake City at
320 South Rio Grande Street just west
of Temple Square. The **Salt Lake International Airport** (801–575–2400) is
7 miles north of
downtown, with
regular shuttles
to major hotels.
The **Church of
Jesus Christ of
Latter-Day
Saints**, as the
Mormon Church
is officially
known, is still a major influence here.
Temple Square (50 West North
Temple Street; 801–240–2534), the
heart of Salt Lake City and the Mormon

■ Grand Teton
National Park was
founded in 1929 only
after the National Park
Service overcame bitter
opposition from ranch-
ers and the U.S. Forest
Service.

church, attracts more than four million visitors annually. The 10-acre site is surrounded by a 15-foot wall and contains the **Salt Lake Temple;** the **Mormon Tabernacle,** home of the **Mormon Tabernacle Choir;** the **Gothic Assembly Hall,** as well as two visitors' centers and other monuments. The nearby **Beehive House,** which served as Brigham Young's home, has been restored and furnished with period furniture (67 East South Temple Street; 801–240–2671). Other city attractions fan out from Temple Square, north to the **Capitol Hill District** and south to shopping and arts locations. The **Utah State Historical Society** is housed in the airy Rio Grande Railroad Depot, featuring life-sized exhibits depicting the pioneer experience (300 South Rio Grande; 801–533–3500; www.history.utah.org). Host city for the **2002 Winter Olympics,** Salt Lake City has also grown into a major winter-sports destination.

One conveniently located downtown hotel is a restored 1900 railroad hotel. The **Peery Hotel** is adjacent to the Salt Palace and some rooms have views of the majestic Wasatch Range (110 West 300 South; 801–521–4300). The **Inn at Temple Square,** owned by the Mormon Church, is a gracious, refurbished hotel that occupies a corner facing Temple Square (71 West South Temple; 801–531–1000).

Earth-toned landscapes form the backdrop as the American Orient Express makes its way to Salt Lake City.

INFORMATION

- **American Orient Express,** 5100 Main Street, Suite 300, Downers Grove, IL 60515; (630) 663–4550 or (888) 759–3944. **E-mail:** sales@americanorientexpress.com. **Web site:** www.americanorientexpress.com.

- **Colorado National Monument,** Fruita, CO 81521; (970) 858–3617. **Web site:** www.nps.gov/colm.

- **Arches National Park,** P.O. Box 907, Moab, UT 84532; (435) 719–2299. **Web site:** www.arches.national-park. com.

- **Grand Teton National Park,** P.O. Drawer 170, Moose, WY 83012; (307) 739–3300. **Web site:** www.nps. gov/grte.

- **Yellowstone National Park,** P.O. Box 168, Yellowstone National Park, WY 82190; (307) 344–7381. **Web site:** www.nps.gov/yell.

- **Denver:** www.milehighcity.com

- **Salt Lake City:** www.visitsaltlake.com

The Canadian Rockies

From the parapets of the Canadian Rocky Mountains to the wild and scenic Pacific Coast, this journey is a unique way to explore the sparsely populated and ruggedly scenic areas of Canada's British Columbia province. The Skeena's route through the Rockies and across the inner plains follows ancient trading routes used by aboriginal peoples, fur trappers, and gold prospectors, and provides the only access to British Columbia's spectacular northern landscapes.

THE TRAIN
The *Skeena*

Known by locals as the "Rupert Rocket," the *Skeena* is one of VIA Rail's premier passenger trains. The gorgeous scenery along the way draws many to take the train. In fact, the *Skeena* used to run as an overnight train, until the railroad wisely decided the route was too beautiful to spend half of it in darkness. An overnight stay in Prince George now allows passengers to see all the scenery.

■ Railway signs along the route offer some insight into the line's history. Newer station name boards are white with a black CN logo and name, mounted on a post. Older station name boards, also white with black lettering, show the name in all capitals, and the sign is mounted on a building.

Popular with rail fans, the *Skeena*'s stainless steel cars were put into service in 1955 and retain the feel of luxury train travel. They've been completely restored in an Art Deco style enhanced by etched glass and original Canadian artwork throughout the train. The *Skeena* offers coach and first-class accommodations. During the peak summer tourist season, the *Skeena* usually carries three passenger cars, with one reserved for coach passengers and two for first-class passengers.

THE ROUTE
Jasper, Alberta ~ Canadian Rockies ~ Prince George, British Columbia ~ Prince Rupert, British Columbia

The *Skeena* travels through some of the most remote and beautiful country in Canada. *Skeena* means "river of mists" in the native Gitksan language, but passengers see much more than the namesake river during this two-day journey. The route crosses 191 bridges and travels through fourteen tunnels, passing snow-capped mountain peaks, glaciers, waterfalls, raging rivers, rich green forests, pristine lakes, and Native American villages complete with totem poles. The *Skeena*'s 725-mile trip takes about twenty hours. Passengers are free to add other stops along the route, which is dotted with small, quaint towns and offers a tremendous diversity of outdoor activities, including **heli-hiking, camping, horseback riding,** and **mountain biking**.

■ Milepost numbers along the *Skeena*'s route rise from east to west, and reset to zero at the start of each subdivision. Subdivisions are 43 to 146 miles long.

Views of imposing Mount Robson are a highlight of the Skeena's journey from Jasper, Alberta to Prince Rupert in British Columbia.

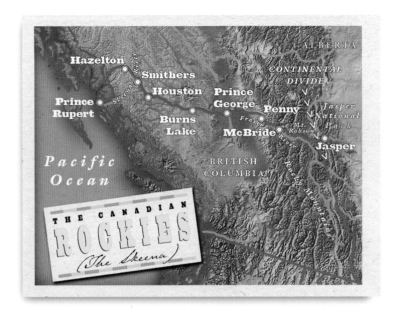

THE CANADIAN ROCKIES

(The Skeena)

Departing from Jasper in early afternoon, the *Skeena* heads westward over Yellowhead Pass and into the Rockies. Soon the Fraser River comes into view, which the train will parallel to Prince George. At 822 miles, the Fraser, a favorite among salmon fishers, is the longest river in British Columbia. The route passes the majestic **Mount Robson,** the highest peak in the Canadian Rockies.

■ Yellowhead Pass marks the border between Alberta and British Columbia and is the highest point of the trip. East of Yellowhead, water flows toward the Arctic Ocean; westward water flows into Yellowhead Lake, en route to the Pacific Ocean.

A graceful, scalloped steel bridge transports the *Skeena* over the Fraser to Prince George, the largest city in northern British Columbia and the crossroad of major north-south and east-west transportation routes. An overnight stay is required here, at the "White Spruce Capital of the World."

Leaving Prince George the next morning, the *Skeena* follows the meandering Nechako River for 75 miles before climbing to the westward expanse of the interior plateau. Occasionally the train slows to allow a bear or moose to cross the tracks. A regular stop is Smithers, a logging town that marks the end of the interior plateau. Here the route parallels the Bulkley River, where passengers often see native fishermen using traditional spear-like gaffs to pluck salmon from the rapids.

At New Hazelton, the train first meets its namesake river, which it will follow all the way to Prince Rupert on the Pacific Coast. As the train enters Prince Rupert, it passes the Alaskan and BC ferry terminals, a reminder that Prince Rupert is a major port for cruise ships heading to Alaska.

The *Skeena* makes the run between Jasper and Prince Rupert three times weekly, with departures on Wednesdays, Fridays, and Saturdays.

ACCOMMODATIONS

Economy service is always available on board the *Skeena,* but passengers traveling during the busy season (mid-May through mid-October) have the option of upgrading to VIA Rail's Totem class. This first-class service includes meals served at your seat and exclusive use of the "Park Car," which features an upper deck with plush seats and panoramic views through a domed ceiling, as well as a downstairs lounge. There is no baggage service, so VIA Rail recommends that passengers restrict themselves to two items of carry-on luggage per person. These items must not exceed 24 inches by 16 inches by 10 inches, or weigh more than fifty pounds.

The rugged landscape of Kitselas Canyon forced railroad builders to construct a series of four tunnels.

RATES

One-way for the first-class Totem service is about $240 (U.S. dollars, depending on current exchange rates) for the two-day trip from Jasper to Prince Rupert. Economy-class tickets are approximately $96. Discounts are available for seniors and children.

WHAT'S INCLUDED: First-class service includes all meals on board.

WHAT'S NOT INCLUDED: For those traveling economy class, sandwiches and snacks may be purchased on board. Gratuities are not included in the fare. The *Skeena* requires an overnight stay in Prince George. Several hotel accommodations are available, but the price is not included in the rail fare. Passengers must make their own reservations. A seven percent Goods & Services Tax (GST) is added to the price, but Canada will refund the GST for nonresidents who fill out the appropriate form.

VIA Rail has a generous refund policy. In most cases refunds are available immediately at any VIA sales office or at the travel agency that arranged for the tickets.

■ It's been said that in other countries, the nation built the railroad, but in Canada, the railroad built the nation. In many parts of Canada, the train was there first, and the people followed.

■ Many of the towns along the *Skeena*'s route are so small that, for the brief moments when the train passes, their populations are doubled or even quadrupled.

ON BOARD

DINING: The *Skeena* prides itself on its regional cuisine and offers Totem-class passengers a continental breakfast and a hot lunch and dinner. Wine is available at dinner only. For economy-class passengers, separate food and beverage service is available throughout the trip. In the peak season, cart service provides sandwiches, snack items, and soft drinks. During the off-peak season, these items are available at the take-out counter in the "Park Car."

DRESS CODE: Casual.

PASSENGERS: The *Skeena* is known as a friendly, informal train and includes passengers from all over the world.

The town of McBride was built during construction of the Grand Trunk Pacific Railroad.

CREW: Each trip has a service manager who provides onboard services and information for passengers. The *Skeena* is known for its friendly staff. Because the train is usually not overly crowded, the conductor often takes time to visit with those on board.

MAJOR STOPS

■ JASPER, ALBERTA: Located near scenic **Jasper National Park** (780–852–6176; www.worldweb.com/ParksCanada-Jasper), the town of Jasper was founded as a major stop on the railroad. Set in one of the preeminent backpacking areas in North America, Jasper has become a major tourist town. Among favorite activities for visitors is a ride on the **Jasper Tramway** (780–852–3093; www.jaspertramway.com), which whisks riders up the steep flank of **Whistlers Mountain.** A cafeteria is at the summit, and trails lead through alpine meadows. The **Jasper-Yellowhead Museum** (400 Pyramid Lake Road; 403–852–3013) has historical exhibits illustrating what the region was like when prospectors and settlers arrived more than a century ago. There are several charming inns in Jasper, including the landmark **Athabasca Hotel,** right in the center of town (780–852–3386).

■ The highest mountain in the Canadian Rockies, Mount Robson is noted for its horizontal strata. The native name for Robson is *Yuh-hai-has-hun,* "Mountain of the Spiral Road."

The Skeena's dome car affords passengers breathtaking panoramic views of the wilderness beyond.

HIGHLIGHT

■ *The stretch of the* Skeena's *route between Smithers and Prince Rupert is flanked by majestic cedar trees. Native Americans used the cedar bark for weaving baskets, mats, and clothes; the trees themselves were used for canoes and shelters, as well as to create totem poles. The area around Hazelton and Kitwanga contains British Columbia's greatest concentration of standing totem poles.*

■ **MCBRIDE, B.C.:** The town of McBride is the only scheduled stop on the route between Jasper and Prince George. Once a busy railroad community of 2,500 inhabitants, McBride lost most of its population when the track construction crews moved on. The **Grand Trunk Pacific Railway Station,** built in 1919, is a reminder of the town's strong railroad history. Nestled in the narrow Robson Valley, McBride now has a population of about 700 and serves the farming, lumbering, and ranching districts of the valley. Nearby is the **Mount Robson Provincial Park** (250–566–4325), which provides a closer look at Mount Robson and some of the most spectacular scenery in the Rockies. There are several lodging choices close to town: **Sandman Inn at McBride** (250–569–2285) and **McBride Travellers Inn** (499 Main Street; 250–569–2609).

■ The *Skeena* passes through Fort Fraser, near the site of a fur trading post built in 1806 by explorer Simon Fraser. The last spike to complete the Grand Trunk Pacific Railway was driven close by in 1914.

■ Five species of salmon are indigenous to the coastal waters of British Columbia. Although some can live for several years, all adult Atlantic salmon die after spawning.

■ **PRINCE GEORGE, B.C.:** The trip on the *Skeena* requires an overnight stay in Prince George, and passengers must make their own arrangements. Among the several hotels available there are the **Best Western City Centre** (910 Victoria Street; 800–528–1234); **Coast Inn of the North** (770 Brunswick Street; 250–563–0121); and the **Ramada Prince George** (444 George Street; 250–563–0055). **BC Bed & Breakfasts Only!** (www.pixsell.bc.ca/bcbbd.htm) has listings for bed and breakfasts in Prince George, or anywhere throughout British Columbia.

Prince George has grown to become the capital of northern British Columbia and is now the third largest city in the province. Its economy is fueled by forest industries. The **Fraser–Fort George Regional Museum** (Twentieth Avenue and Gorse Street; 250–562–1612; www.museum.princegeorge.com) in Fort George Park features artifacts illustrating the local history of the area. Train buffs should leave time for the **Central British Columbia Railway and Forest Industry Museum,** located next to the rail yards (850 River Road; 250–563–7351;www.pgrfm.bc.ca). This museum offers a collection of photos and railcars and traces the history of the region since the arrival of the railroad.

■ **SMITHERS, B.C.:** Built on an ancient lake bed, Smithers offers many outdoor adventures. **Year-round skiing** is available, as is **mountain climbing** and **fishing** for salmon or steelhead. The **Smithers Visitor Information Center** (1411 Court Street; 800–542–6673 or 250–847–5072) has information on area attractions. The most popular tourist site is **Twin Falls** (off Route 16), which features spectacular twin waterfalls cascading down canyon walls. In the winter, climbers have been known to scale the frozen waterfalls. For those wanting to spend a night in Smithers, among the hotels in town is the **Stork Nest Inn** (1485 Main Street; 250–847–3831), located right next to the Visitor Information Center.

■ **PRINCE RUPERT, B.C.:** Prince Rupert is the transport hub for British Columbia's north coast. Its other major industries are commercial fishing, seafood processing, and wood-pulp processing. The **Kwinitsa Railway Museum**

■ Salmon hatch in freshwater and remain there for up to 18 months before moving into the ocean. Salmon have a remarkable migratory instinct. Each generation returns to spawn in exactly the same breeding places as the generation before, often struggling for miles against a river's strong currents.

(Waterfront Park; 250–627–1915), featuring railway artifacts and videos, is located on the waterfront in an original rail station brought to Prince Rupert by barge in 1985. Travelers wishing to stay near the train station in the downtown area have several choices of accommodations, including the **Best Western Highliner Inn** (815 First Avenue West; 250–624–9060) and the **Moby Dick Inn** (935 Second Avenue West; 250–624–6961).

INFORMATION

■ **VIA Rail Canada,** P.O. Box 8116, Station A, Montreal, Quebec H3C 3N3; (888) VIARAIL. **Web site:** www.viarail.ca.

■ **Jasper:** www.visit-jasper.com

■ **Prince George:** www.city.pg.bc.ca

■ **Prince Rupert:** www.rupert.bc.ca

■ **British Columbia Tourism:** www.travel.bc.ca

The Skeena's tracks skirt the shoreline of Moose Lake.

The Coast Starlight

The Coast Starlight *runs on Amtrak's
flagship route and has been pampered and preened
with restoration work during the past few years. The
goal—to provide what Amtrak calls a "premier land cruise
travel experience." The makings for a memorable trip are
certainly in place: From the rugged Pacific Coast through
the towering Cascades to the serenity of Puget Sound, the
rails provide an outstanding variety of magnificent views.*

THE TRAIN
Amtrak's *Coast Starlight*

Passengers travel the 1,400 miles between Los Angeles and Seattle
on board Amtrak's Superliner II fleet. First-class status comes with
sleeper accommodations. Coach cars feature upper-level seating with
sweeping views. All cars have big windows and generous aisles as well
as overhead reading lights, fold-down trays, and luggage racks.

Amtrak's extras enhance the trip. The "Sightseer" lounge car's
wraparound picture windows and interpretive guides provide historic
and cultural highlights along the way. In the evening, the "Sightseer"
converts to a movie theater for first-run movies. Amtrak also designed
a new "Kiddie" car with its youngest passengers in mind. The "Pacific
Parlour" car, a modified Heritage Santa Fe high-level car, is reserved
for first-class passengers. Recently refurbished, this car features lounge
chairs and booths for taking in the scenery. The lower level of the
"Parlour" car houses another movie setup, this one complete with
surround-sound audio.

THE ROUTE
Los Angeles ~ Seattle

The *Coast Starlight* runs daily, with morning departures from both Los
Angeles and Seattle. The complete trip takes about thiry-six hours,
with more than two dozen stops in between, allowing plenty of
opportunities for passengers to add side trips to their itineraries.

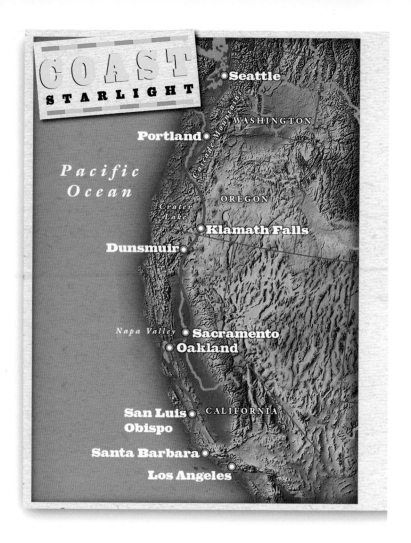

Leaving Los Angeles at about 9:30 A.M., the train travels through the San Fernando Valley before entering the Santa Monica Mountains. A series of tunnels leads to agricultural areas on the way to the coast, first glimpsed upon arrival in Ventura. For the next four hours, the train hugs the spectacular California coastline. After a stop in Santa Barbara, the route's path between mountains and ocean continues for several hours, offering glimpses of seals and sea lions in the **Channel Islands,** a fragile and beautiful refuge for rare species of plants and animals.

■ The *Coast Starlight* makes a stop in Martinez, California, the connecting point for Amtrak trains serving the cities in the San Joaquin Valley.

The *Coast Starlight* heads inland at Point Purisima to San Luis Obispo. Shortly after leaving this quaint town, passengers have a terrific opportunity to see the entire train wrapped around two spectacular horseshoe curves at **Cuesta Pass,** a highlight of the trip.

The *Coast Starlight* reaches the San Francisco/Oakland area as evening descends, making its inland journey through Sacramento and northern California during the night. In the morning the train heads into the rugged foothills of the **Cascade Mountains** in Oregon. Once crossing the border, high mountain peaks come into view, culminating in the cluster that frames **Crater Lake,** one of Oregon's top tourist attractions. The next three hours through the heart of the Cascades are packed with spectacular mountain views, most of which can only be seen from the train. Once across the divide at Willamette Pass, the twisting switchback tracks descend 3,500 feet. Thrilled passengers enjoy 50 miles of clinging to the steep cliffs of the canyon wall. Civilization returns as the train nears Eugene and then heads into the **Willamette Valley,** Oregon's wine country. Clear days provide a view of **Mount Hood** as the train approaches Portland's Union Station. Weather permitting, passengers can see **Mount St. Helens** shortly after the train stops in Longview. During the afternoon, the train follows the old stagecoach route between Portland and Seattle. Pulling into Olympia at about 6:30 P.M., the route follows Puget Sound for the remainder of the trip, which affords excellent views of **Mount Rainier** between Olympia and Tacoma. About ninety minutes after leaving Tacoma, the *Coast Starlight* arrives in Seattle, its final destination.

ACCOMMODATIONS

The *Coast Starlight* offers both coach and first-class accommodations. The seats in coach cars are spacious, recline fully, and include folding leg rests. First-class passengers have a choice of private sleeping compartments. The **Standard Bedroom,** which has shared bath facilities, can accommodate one or two people. The **Deluxe Bedroom** includes private bath facilities, upper-level views, an armchair, and a sofa. Dual-level beds can sleep two to three adults. The **Family Bedroom,** for up to two adults and two children, is spacious and takes up the full width of the train providing views on both sides; bathroom facilities are shared. An **Accessible Bedroom** for passengers with special needs features ample room for a wheelchair and a private toilet. An attendant is on hand in each car to help with baggage, answer questions, and, if asked, bring passengers breakfast in bed.

Oregon's Crater Lake lies in the center of an extinct volcano. At 1,932 feet it is the deepest lake in the United States.

RATES

Passengers pay a rail fare for every person traveling; any sleeping accommodation is an extra one-time charge. Both rail fare and sleeper fares vary depending on season and availability. The rail fare between Los Angeles and Seattle can be as low as $101 per person or as high as $168. A Standard Bedroom runs between $235 and $321; Deluxe Bedroom between $510 and $728. The range for the Family Bedroom is $433 to $618. The Accessible Bedroom starts at $326 and can go as high as $464. As on all Amtrak trains, children under the age of 2 travel free. Two children between the ages of 2 and 15 may travel at half the rail fare with an adult. A fifteen-percent discount is given to senior citizens over the age of 62. Reservations are required.

Passengers wanting to stop and visit cities along the way should look into Amtrak's Explore America Fare or ask a ticket agent about other options. Most tickets are refundable before travel begins, but a fee applies in most cases. Some discount tickets may be nonrefundable once issued.

WHAT'S INCLUDED: First-class rail fare includes five full meals; baggage handling is included for all passengers.

WHAT'S NOT INCLUDED: Food service in coach and gratuities are extra.

■ The naming of sleeping cars was a time-honored Pullman tradition. While the practice has largely ceased, Amtrak has named its Superliner II sleeping cars after states in which the trains operate.

ON BOARD

DINING: The dining car features master chefs who prepare fresh meals daily, showcasing specialties from regions along the route. Entrees include Oregon Trail Salmon Filet, Castroville Cheese Tortellini, and Mount Hood Baked Chicken. Meals are served with wines selected from vintners in California, Oregon, and Washington to capture the local flavors. First-class passengers are treated to afternoon wine-tasting receptions with fresh fruit and cheeses.

More casual dining options are available in the lower-level cafe bar, which serves sandwiches, snacks, and beverages. Attendants are also happy to bring a meal to coach seating or a sleeping cabin.

DRESS CODE: Casual

Passengers enjoy the wraparound picture windows of the "Sightseer" lounge car.

PASSENGERS: Amtrak is clearly ready to welcome families on board the *Coast Starlight.* The new "Kiddie" car makes it easy to keep little ones entertained. The crew also occasionally announces games for children in the "Sightseer" lounge.

■ Los Angeles's Union Station has been called the last of America's great train stations. A rich blend of Spanish and Art Deco styles, it was completed in 1939 just as passenger rail travel started to fade.

■ The *Coast Starlight* passes through restricted areas of the Vandenberg Air Force Base, home to the Strategic Air Command's Western Missile Test Range, and the launch site for military missiles and satellites.

CREW: *Coast Starlight* crew members go through special training to boost customer service. Amtrak offers a guarantee that if a guest's onboard experience doesn't meet expectations, the guest receives a free travel credit for another trip.

MAJOR STOPS

■ **LOS ANGELES:** Los Angeles's **Union Station** is located at 800 North Alameda Street. Directly across from Union Station is the 44-acre **El Pueblo de Los Angeles Historical Monument,** a state park that commemorates the site where the city was founded in 1781. Many early buildings are preserved here, but the central attraction for most is **Olvera Street,** a Mexican-style marketplace teeming with restaurants, shops, and stalls of vendors selling Mexican crafts. (The Visitors Center is located at 622 North Main Street; 213–628–1274; www.cityofla.org/ELP.)

Families with young children might be interested in a visit to the **Travel Town Museum,** located in Griffith Park (5200 Zoo Drive; 213–662–5874). Boasting a collection of fourteen steam loco-

HIGHLIGHT

■ *Amtrak has recently added a "Kiddie" car to its West Coast repertoire. The modified, bi-level Superliner II coach sports colorful benches and a large collection of blocks, trucks, and other toys, as well as stuffed animals and dolls. Open from 7:00 A.M. to 10:00 P.M., the car is also equipped with a video monitor for cartoons and movies. While it sounds like fun, the welcoming sign makes clear this car is for a restricted ridership:* ALL PARENTS MUST BE ACCOMPANIED BY CHILDREN.

motives, Travel Town was envisioned as a "railroad petting zoo" when it was founded in the 1940s. The museum now features a 16-inch gauge train that came from Gene Autry's Melody Ranch in Saugus, California. Griffith Park is also home to the **Los Angeles Zoo** (213–666–4090) and the **Planetarium and Observatory** (213–664–1191).

For just twenty-five cents, passengers can ride the city's famed **Angels Flight** funicular railway at 351 South Hill Street between Third and Fourth Streets. Originally built in 1901, it is known as "The World's Shortest Railway," with its two counterbalanced passenger cars ascending and descending the hill. The restored funicular uses the original railcars, the station house, and the two end station arches. Fares are collected at the top. *Angels Flight* connects downtown L.A.'s historic district with the modern financial district at the top of the hill. The endpoint is the **California Plaza Watercourt,** featuring shops, restaurants, and a public live entertainment space highlighted by water-jet displays. The California Plaza complex also houses the **Museum of Contemporary Art** (250 South Grand Avenue; 213–626–6222; www.moca-la.org), as well as the **Hotel Intercontinental** (251 South Olive Street; 213–617–3300). For the ultimate in luxury in downtown L.A., there is the **Regal Biltmore,** a Spanish

Italian Renaissance beauty from the 1920s that has been designated an Historical Cultural Landmark (506 South Grand Avenue; 213–624–1011; www.thebiltmore.com). There are also numerous hotels near **Los Angeles International Airport** (310–646–5252), which is located about 25 miles west of downtown.

■ **OAKLAND:** One of the most popular side trips from the *Coast Starlight* is to California wine country, and rail buffs can enjoy the experience by rail. The **Napa Valley Wine Train** (800–427–4124; www.winetrain.com) is a three-hour excursion on board beautifully restored train cars, including a Dome Vista car and a 1917 vintage

■ Mount Rainier is one of the great scenic wonders of the Pacific Northwest. A dormant volcano towering 14,410 feet, its peak is perpetually capped in snow. Twenty-six glaciers flow from its summit.

Pullman dining car. The trip features excellent California cuisine and, of course, a chance to taste fine wines from the region. Passengers wishing to take this side trip get off the *Coast Starlight* at Oakland, California, where Amtrak's new station is located in the heart of **Jack London Square** (510–814–6000; www.jacklondonsq.com). There are numerous clubs, restaurants, and shops in this district, which overlooks San Francisco Bay. There are several places to stay right in the square itself, including the luxurious **Waterfront Plaza Hotel** (10 Washington Street; 510–836–3800). For something out of the ordinary, visitors can arrange with **Dockside**

If the weather cooperates, the Coast Starlight *provides stunning views of several famous mountain peaks, including Mount Rainier.*

Boat and Bed to spend an evening aboard a yacht right along the square (419 Water Street; 510–444–5858; www.boatandbed.com). Travelers who want to spend a night in Napa Valley can contact the **Napa Valley Conference & Visitors Bureau** (707–226–7459; www.napavalley.com) for a complete list of area accommodations.

■ **SACRAMENTO:** Although the *Coast Starlight* pulls into Sacramento around midnight, train enthusiasts should consider staying for a longer visit. Just one block from the Amtrak station is the **California State Railroad Museum** (111 I Street; 916–445–7387; www.scrmf.org). Considered the largest interpretative railroad museum in the world, it is located in a 23-acre state park between Interstate 5 and the Sacramento River known as **Old Sacramento** (916–264–7031; www.oldsacramento.com). Offering a variety of shopping, dining, and entertainment, this historic enclave also houses the **Discovery Museum of History, Science, and Technology** (101 I Street; 916–264–7057; www.thediscovery.org), the **California Military Museum** (1119 Second Street; 916–442–2883; www.militarymuseum.org), and the **Wells Fargo History Museum** (1000 Second Street; 916–440–4263; www.wellsfargo.com/about/museum/info).

Those wanting to stay in Old Sacramento have the option of spending the night on an old-time paddlewheeler. The *Delta King,* sister ship to the better-known Mississippi River cruiser *Delta Queen,* once transported people and goods between San Francisco and Sacramento. The riverboat has now been converted into an upscale hotel (1000 Front Street; 800–825–5464; www.deltaking.com). Two other riverboats—the *Spirit of Sacramento* and the *Matthew McKinley*—still offer a variety of trips along the Sacramento River (110 L Street; 800–433–0263; www.oldsacriverboat.com).

■ One of Santa Barbara's landmarks stands just to the left of the station—an old Moreton Bay fig tree planted in 1877. With a spread of 160 feet, it's the largest tree of its kind in the country.

■ **PORTLAND, OR:** Portland is well known for its extensive park system, which includes **Washington Park,** home of the famous **International Rose Test Gardens** (400 Southwest Kingston; 503–823–3636), and **Forest Park,** which houses the **Oregon Zoo** (4001 Southwest Canyon Road; 503–226–1561; www.zooregon.org). Visitors to the zoo can take a ride on the **Washington Park and Zoo Railway,** which offers scenic views of downtown Portland, Mount Hood, and Mount St. Helens. The line's three trains were built to scale, five-sixths the size of the old narrow-gauge railways. Washington Park is also home to Portland's **Japanese Garden,** well known for its displays of five formal garden styles (611 Southwest Kingston Avenue; 503–223–1321). Portland's historic old town offers many restaurants, galleries, and museums. The **Oregon History Center** (1200

The Coast Starlight's route travels more than a hundred miles along the spectacular beaches of the California coastline.

■ Amtrak recommends medium-speed film for shooting scenery through train windows. Holding the camera lens close to the window helps eliminate glare and reflections.

■ Many people passing through the Salinas Valley think the large plants along the tracks are weeds. They're actually artichokes. Castroville is known as the Artichoke Capital of the World.

Southwest Park Avenue; 503–222–1741; www.ohs.org), easily recognized by its eight-story-high trompe l'oeil murals, features interactive exhibits depicting the history of the region. Portland's historic **Union Station,** opened in 1896, is located in the heart of downtown (800 Northwest Sixth Avenue; 503–273–4865). A good place to start is the **Visitor Information and Services Center** at the corner of Southwest Naito Parkway and Salmon Street (503–222–2223 or 87–PORTLAND; www.pova.com), which provides brochures, maps, and ticketing services.

There are many fine hotels in downtown Portland and the **Oregon Bed and Breakfast Guild** can offer suggestions on B&Bs in the area (800–944–6196; www.obbg.org).

■ **SEATTLE:** Amtrak's station in Seattle is located downtown at 303 South Jackson Street, about 13 miles from **Seattle-Tacoma**

■ Some of the tunnels the train passes through as it descends from the Cascade Mountains are actually snow sheds built to protect the tracks from snow accumulations.

International Airport (206–431–4444) and nearby **Pioneer Square,** a trendy neighborhood of restaurants and galleries. A required stop on a Seattle tour is **Pike Place Market,** a seven-acre hodgepodge of food stalls, craft booths, and street performers. It is the oldest continually operating farmers market in the country (First Avenue at Pike Street; 206–682–7453; www.pikeplacemarket.com).

There are numerous hotels in the downtown area, some with a distinctively Seattle feel. **The Pioneer Square Hotel** features restored turn-of-the-century rooms overlooking Pioneer Square (77 Yesler Way; 206–340–1234; www.pioneersquare.com). Housed in a restored 1901 building near the waterfront, the **Alexis Hotel** is an intimate hotel where some rooms have their own wood-burning fireplaces (1007 First Avenue; 206–624–4844; www.alexishotel.com). The hotel's **Bookstore Bar & Café,** with its floor-to-ceiling bookcases, is a favorite with locals.

Passengers wishing to continue their train experience should consider *The Spirit of Washington* dinner train (800–876–RAIL; www.columbiawinery.com/train). The train's vintage railcars leave from nearby Renton on a three-and-a-half-hour trip around **Lake Washington,** showcasing scenic views of the **Puget Sound** region, the **Olympic Mountains,** the **Seattle Skyline,** and **Mount Rainier.**

INFORMATION

■ **Amtrak,** 530 Water Street, Fifth Floor, Oakland, CA 94607–3746; (800) USA–RAIL or contact local travel agents. **E-Mail:** service@sales.amtrak.com. **Web site:** www.amtrak.com.

■ **Los Angeles:** www.at-la.com

■ **Oakland, CA:** www.oaklandca.com

■ **Napa Valley:** www.napavalley.com

■ **Sacramento:** www.cityofsacramento.org

■ **Portland:** www.pova.com

■ **Seattle:** www.seeseattle.org

The American South by Rail

The American South unfolds its beauty and tradition when seen from a train, which provides a close-up view of the region's back roads and historic cities. Seven days and six nights on the luxurious American Orient Express *offer just such an opportunity. From hospitable Southern cities and antebellum estates draped in Spanish moss to landmarks of Civil War–era Virginia, this route is steeped in the flavor of the Old South.*

THE TRAIN
American Orient Express

America's premier luxury train, the *American Orient Express* is a deluxe vintage assemblage of cars that pay homage to the romantic Streamliner Era. Aiming to be a first-class hotel on wheels, the *American Orient Express* makes sure its passengers travel in indulgent comfort. The vintage cars of the *AOE* were collected from throughout the country and painstakingly restored in 1988 at a cost of $15 million. Now the cars sparkle with polished brass and luxurious leather, mahogany paneling and vintage artwork.

■ For those who want to chart their own rail course, Amtrak serves many of the destinations visited on this *AOE* trip. Amtrak isn't as luxurious, but there's more freedom in forming your own itinerary.

The historic "New York" observation car served the New York Central's famous *20th Century Limited* between New York and Chicago. Its bay window and horseshoe-shaped bar highlight one of the train's favorite gathering places. Club cars feature live piano music and plush seating. Meals are served in style in the train's two formal dining cars, originally built for the Union Pacific Railroad.

The *AOE*'s five sleeper cars offer modern comforts such as air-conditioning and private lavatories. Each carriage has a friendly porter

who provides needed assistance, converts the cabins into beds with crisp linens at the end of the day, schedules the use of the carriage's shower, and offers a fluffy robe and fresh towels to every traveler.

THE ROUTE
New Orleans ~ St. Augustine ~ Savannah ~ Charleston ~ Richmond ~ Washington, D.C.

During the course of the week, *American Orient Express* passengers experience both the vast expanses of the Southern landscape as well as some of its most noted 18th- and 19th-century homes and gardens. Although *AOE* regularly changes the specific stops on this trip to reflect different Southern themes, the basic route remains the same.

The journey begins in the Big Easy. Because this route runs only in the spring, New Orleans is alive with the energy of Mardi Gras. When the time comes to board the train at the **Union Passenger Terminal,** the friendly staff provides a welcoming reception. Dinner is served as the train pulls out of New Orleans and enters the watery landscape of southern Louisiana and Mississippi.

The next day's destination is St. Augustine, Florida, the oldest city in North America. The train parks in Jacksonville, and motor coaches make the hour-long trip to St. Augustine. A sparkling city on the Atlantic coast, it is sometimes compared to a picturesque European village. One of the stops on the tour is the **Lightner**

A visit to Savannah's Historic District is a highlight of this southern swing.

Museum (75 King Street; 904–824–2874), housed in a former grand hotel built by Henry Flagler. Today the museum features a collection of 19th-century decorative arts.

After motoring back to the waiting train, passengers dine on board as the journey moves north to the cobblestone streets and moss-draped oaks of Savannah, Georgia. The train overnights in Savannah, and the next day guides lead a trolley tour through the town's **historic district,** pointing out its impressive Greek Revival, Gothic, and baroque architecture. The tour makes a special call at the 1816 **Owens Thomas House** (124 Abercorn Street; 912–233–9743), an English Regency structure with period rooms brimming in art and collectibles. After lunch at a private home, the tour heads to Savannah's charming waterfront district and then on to the **Fort Pulaski National Monument** (U.S. Highway 80 East; 912–786–5787; www.nps. gov/fopu), a moated fortress that played a major role in the American Revolution, the War of 1812, and the Civil War. Dinner is on board the train, and after another night parked in the Savannah station, the train heads to Charleston as breakfast is served.

■ The city of Savannah claims more than 1,000 restored and preserved buildings in its famed Historic District, set off by the ever-present squares that form its neighborhoods.

Prior to an afternoon spent exploring Charleston, passengers travel a short distance through swamp and cypress low country to **Drayton Hall** (3380 Ashley River Road; 843–766–0188), one of America's finest examples of Georgian-Palladian architecture. The tour then heads up the river to majestic **Middleton Place** (4300 Ashley River Road; 843–556–6020; www.middletonplace .org) home to the nation's oldest landscaped garden. The group lunches at Middleton before heading to Charleston's historic district. Once a prospering seaport, Charleston has worked hard to preserve the stunning evidence of its wealth and sophistication.

The train pulls out of Charleston early the next morning, headed for Richmond, Virginia, capital of the Confederacy. Upon arrival at Richmond, train buffs are in for a special treat as the train pulls into one of the last great monumental train stations built before the Depression. No longer used for daily train travel, but recently renovated, the Neoclassical Revival building now houses the **Science Museum of Virginia** (2500 West Broad Street; 800–367–6552; www.smv.org). Early the next morning, motor coaches head to Charlottesville, where visitors enjoy a private tour of Thomas Jefferson's innovative home, **Monticello** (931 Thomas Jefferson Parkway; 843–984–9822; www.monticello.org). Later the group tours the **University of Virginia,** which Jefferson founded and designed. The trip back to Richmond includes a brief tour of the **Richmond Battlefield Center,** which reflects the area's historic role in the Civil and Revolutionary Wars. After a bus tour of Richmond's historic district, a farewell dinner awaits on board the train, which again spends the night parked at the Broad Street Station.

■ While Union troops destroyed most of the plantation houses in the Ashley River area, Drayton Hall was spared. Drayton is shown unfurnished to highlight its architectural details.

The next morning, the train makes a final two-hour trek through the fertile Shenandoah Valley, before arriving at

One of the South's most historic plantations, Middleton Place features exquisite formal gardens.

■ One hundred slaves built the gardens and pools at Middleton Place over a ten-year period. Today Middleton makes a point of stressing the contributions of the labor and lives of enslaved Africans.

Washington, D.C.'s Union Station. At this point, passengers may be tempted to turn around and make the journey south again. The train does exactly that the next day, offering this itinerary in reverse. *AOE* takes this journey six times every year in March and April, three times in each direction.

ACCOMMODATIONS

Several carriage options are offered, all featuring large picture windows, private lavatories, and hot and cold running water. Standard **Vintage Pullman** compartments have an upper and lower berth and a full-size couch. A **Single Sleeper** provides a lower berth and a single sofa seat. The larger **Parlor Suite** offers two lower berths, a full

couch, and a single sofa seat, as well as an extra upper berth that can be used for a third passenger. For top-of-the-line luxury, there's the **Presidential Suite,** a double-size cabin with two lower berths, two single sofa seats, and its own shower.

RATES

Six nights aboard the *AOE,* prices per person, based on double occupancy: Vintage Pullman: $2490; Single Sleeper: $3590; Parlor Suite: $3,990; Presidential Suite: $4,690. *AOE* recommends you plan early, and offers small discounts to those reserving six months in advance. A $500 deposit is required when booking; $250 of that is refundable until 60 days before departure.

WHAT'S INCLUDED: All nights aboard the *American Orient Express;* welcome and farewell receptions; all meals; soft drinks, bottled water, and house wine with dinner; all excursions and other group activities; lectures and presentations; baggage handling; gratuities to guides, escorts, and drivers; complimentary toiletries package.

WHAT'S NOT INCLUDED: Taxes; transportation to and from the train; accident, baggage, and/or cancellation insurance; personal expenses such as laundry, telephone, fax charges, or taxis; liquor; traditional gratuities to train staff.

ON BOARD

DINING: The *AOE* chefs manage to prepare delicious, creative cuisine in two small galley kitchens, using only the finest local ingredients to create regional specialties and traditional dishes handed down from train chefs of the past. Open seating and leisurely dinner hours allow passengers to relax and enjoy the scenery as they dine.

The chefs typically offer five entree selections for dinners, including traditional and exotic dishes. They are more than willing to accommodate vegetarians or those with dietary restrictions. Tables are set with linen, china, and crystal. The waiters offer a complementary selection of fine wines.

In the morning, passengers can choose a continental breakfast in one of the club cars or a full breakfast in the dining cars, both featuring breads fresh from the oven. Grits are a natural on this southern swing. When touring during the day, the staff takes care to choose atmospheric local restaurants that serve regional cuisine. The train's plush club cars offer morning coffee with continental breakfast, afternoon tea with fine pastries, and cocktails in the evening.

■ The book *Midnight in the Garden of Good and Evil* brought such attention to the Bird Girl statue on its cover that the statue had to be moved out of Bonaventure Cemetery to Savannah's **Telfair Museum of Art** (121 Barnard Street; 912–232–1177; www.telfair.org).

■ America's first passenger train operated on Christmas Day, 1830, in Charleston, South Carolina. Today visitors can view a replica of this train at Charleston's **Best Friend Museum and Shop** (456 King Street; 843–973–7269) near the Visitor Center.

DRESS CODE: The *American Orient Express* advises bringing casual, comfortable clothes. Dresses and jackets are not required in the evening or at dinner.

PASSENGERS: The number of passengers is limited to 108, and the crew makes a point to foster a congenial, clubby atmosphere. Though the pace of the trip is not suitable for young children, the company says they are beginning to see an increasing number of older children and teens traveling with parents or grandparents. Because the group tours do involve walking and climbing stairs, *AOE* expects passengers to be in good health and to enjoy traveling with others.

CREW: Expert guides and lecturers are on board to provide historical, cultural, and scientific insights throughout the trip and its land excursions.

MAJOR STOPS

■ **NEW ORLEANS:** The New Orleans **Union Passenger Terminal** (504–528–1610) is located at 1001 Loyola Avenue in the **Central Business District,** near the **Superdome.** The **New Orleans International Airport** (504–464–0831) is 15 miles west of the city in Kenner via the Earhart Expressway.

Ebullient New Orleans is a delight for the senses. Eyes feast on

HIGHLIGHT

■ *The 10-square blocks of New Orleans's French Quarter represent America's premier partying place, where visitors are surrounded by sights, sounds, smells, and tastes that are the essence of this spirited city. The French Quarter—or Vieux Carré (meaning "old square")—was established in 1718 by the French as a military outpost. When the Spanish acquired New Orleans in 1763, the two cultures melded with strong influences from the African slave population to form the famous Creole society and cuisine for which New Orleans is so well known. Today, from bawdy Bourbon Street to the secluded courtyards on elegant side streets, the French Quarter still exudes native culture and old-world character.*

the architectural beauty of the **French Quarter** (www.frenchquarter. com) and the graceful homes of the **Garden District;** ears revel in the jazz, blues, or zydeco that rises from the street corners or drifts from the nightclubs. Delicious smells are in the air, and the French and Creole cuisine, among others, combine to assure a deliciously decadent dining experience. The **French Market** (between Decatur and North Peters Streets), a New Orleans institution since 1790, is often the first stop for *AOE* chefs, who stock up on the Creole and Cajun ingredients that give their meals on this trip a Southern flair. Two of New Orleans's most elegant hotels are located near the French Quarter and the Union Passenger Terminal: the **Pelham Hotel** (444 Common Street; 888–856–4486; www.thepelhamhotel.com) and the **Lafayette Hotel** (600 St. Charles Avenue; 888–856–4706; www.thelafayettehotel.com). Travelers wanting more intimate accommodations can contact **New Orleans Bed and Breakfast** (P.O. Box 8163, New Orleans, LA 70182; 504–838–0071; www.neworleansbandb.com).

■ You'll need to wash quickly aboard the *AOE*. The train observes the railroad tradition of no more than three minutes in the shower, ensuring that there is always plenty of hot water for each passenger.

■ **ST. AUGUSTINE:** In 1565, Don Pedro Menéndez de Avilés founded St. Augustine, drawn by the fact that it was surrounded on three sides by rivers and could be protected on the fourth by a fort. Today, the city exudes charm and history. Its **Castillo de San Marcos** fort is now a national monument

■ In the heyday of America's luxury trains, paint on the cars was varnished to make it shiny. The word "varnish" is still slang for a first-class passenger car.

(One South Castillo Drive; 904–829–6506; www.nps.gov/casa). The city's **Spanish Quarter** (904–824–8874) has been reconstructed into a historic village museum, where horse-drawn carriages traverse narrow streets and people dressed in period costumes explain what life was like for colonists in a garrison town. For those seeking eternal youth, a visit to the **Fountain of Youth** may be in order; visitors can drink from the spring discovered by Ponce de Leon in 1513 (Fountain of Youth National Archaeological Park, 11 Magnolia Avenue; 904–829–3168).

■ **SAVANNAH:** Savannah is the quintessential small Southern city, its live oaks draped in Spanish moss, its Georgian row houses lovingly preserved in neighborhoods built around charming public squares. Savannah claims to be America's first planned city. The **historic wharf** district is now predominately occupied by restaurants, antiques shops, and boutiques.

■ **CHARLESTON, S.C.:** Charleston remains one of the most hospitable and best-preserved cities in the Old South. A host of carefully tended pre-Revolutionary buildings and stately homes from antebellum days take visitors back to a forgotten era. The city also played an

Many of Savannah's historic buildings have been restored using original paint colors—pinks, reds, blues, and greens.

Passengers are treated to gourmet cuisine with a regional flair in the train's beautifully restored dining cars.

important role in America's history. The first engagement of the Civil War took place in April of 1861 at **Fort Sumter** (843–722–1691; ww.nps.gov/fosu), which has since become a national monument.

■ **RICHMOND:** Compared to many Southern cities, Richmond is relatively young. Although founded in 1607, it had to re-create itself after much of the city was burned to the ground in 1865, one reason the Civil War holds such a prominent place in the city's history. The city's **Museum of the Confederacy** (1201 East Clay Street; 843–649–1861; www.moc.org) contains an extensive collection of military and political artifacts from the Confederate period. The museum complex also includes the **White House of the Confederacy,** which was the official residence of Confederate president Jefferson Davis.

■ **WASHINGTON, D.C.:** Washington's **Union Station** is located at 50 Massachusetts Avenue NE (www.unionstation.com), not far from the **Capitol Building. Ronald Reagan Washington National Airport** is about 15 minutes away just across the Potomac; **Dulles International Airport** is 45 minutes west of downtown via I–66 (www.metwashairports.com). **Baltimore-Washington International Airport** (www.bwiairport.com) is also about forty-five minutes away, near Baltimore to the northeast of Washington. Frequent shuttles service all three airports, as does the Metro.

Among Washington's many popular tourist attractions, the Smithsonian's **National Museum of American History** at Constitution Avenue and Fourteenth Street (202–357–2700; www.american history.si.edu) is of special interest to rail enthusiasts. Railroad Hall features locomotives dating from the 1850s through the 1920s, an electric streetcar, and many other artifacts and models that help tell the history of the railroad.

■ George Pullman came up with the idea of the sleeper car in 1867 with the help of Andrew Carnegie. That same year, George Westinghouse patented the air brake, and the refrigerator car was developed.

Lodging is plentiful in Washington. Two of the most famous, the **Hotel Washington** (Pennsylvania Avenue at Fifteenth Street; 202–638–5900; www. hotelwashington.com) and the **Hay Adams Hotel** (One Lafayette Square; 202–638–6600; www.hayadams.com) are located near the **White House** and the attractions on the **Mall**. On a smaller scale, many **bed and breakfasts** are scattered throughout the metropolitan area (Bed & Breakfast Accommodations, Ltd., P.O. Box 12011, Washington, DC 20005; 202–328–3510; www. bnbaccom.com).

INFORMATION

■ **American Orient Express**, 5100 Main Street, Suite 300, Downers Grove, IL 60515; (800) 759–3944 or 630–663–1595. **E-Mail:** sales@americanorientexpress.com. **Web site:** www.americanorientexpress.com.

■ **New Orleans:** www.neworleans.com

■ **St. Augustine:** www.oldcity.com

■ **Savannah:** www.savannah-visit.com

■ **Charleston:** www.charlestoncvb.com

■ **Richmond:** www.ci.richmond.va.us

■ **Washington, D.C.:** www.ci.washington.dc.us

Alaska's Gold Rush Train

They built it quickly and against all odds, through seemingly impossibly rugged terrain, but there was gold in them thar' hills, and prospectors during Alaska's 1898 Klondike Gold Rush had dreams of fortune. Today, the White Pass & Yukon Route *provides a trip back in time on refurbished train cars that follow the original route of those hopeful stampeders.*

THE TRAIN
The *White Pass & Yukon Route Railway*

An ever-present sense of history is responsible for much of the magic of this trip. The discovery of gold in the Klondike started one of history's most remarkable stampedes of people. In 1897, the first year of the gold rush, up to 30,000 people crossed the two perilous White Pass and Chilkoot trails into Canada. Few realized the hardships they would face just getting to this promised land. Conditions were harsh and the trails arduous. Still, thousands of miners, some with wives and children in tow, set off on the journey. The trip was made even more difficult when, after the starvation deaths of early prospectors, the Northwest Mounted Police started standing guard at White Pass Summit, turning back anyone not fully equipped with a year's supplies, which weighed roughly a ton.

■ Engineers say modern-day aerial surveys of the *White Pass Railroad* tracks show that no better route could have been forged through the mountains than the one chosen in 1898 from surveys done on foot.

The *White Pass & Yukon Route Railway* offers one of the last remaining opportunities to ride on a narrow-gauge railway in the United States, retracing the path of those frantic gold seekers. More than fifty railcars operate on the line. Some are restored parlor cars

straight out of the 1890s, with their polished green and brass exteriors, while others have been built in just the last few years to vintage specifications.

The pride and joy of the line is Steam Engine No. 73, a restored 1947, 2–8–2 Mikado-class Baldwin locomotive that proudly escorts most trains to the edge of Skagway and sends them on their way. The *White Pass Railroad* is leasing Steam Engine No. 40, a 1920 Baldwin 2–8–0 from Colorado's Georgetown Loop Railroad for the next five years. The *WP&YR*'s roster also includes ten General Electric and nine Alco diesel locomotives.

THE ROUTE
Skagway ~ White Pass Summit

WP&YR uses the same rail line that carried Gold Rush stampeders, though the trip is now much shorter. The *White Pass & Yukon Route Railroad* originally ran from Skagway to Whitehorse, Yukon. Only 40 miles of the original 110 are in use today, although tracks still run the full length of the route. The company is upgrading some rails farther north and may eventually extend the trip as far as Carcross at milepost 67.

Several trip options are offered, the most popular is a three-hour guided excursion to **White Pass Summit.** Other outings take passengers farther, such as an eight-and-a-half-hour trip to **Lake Bennett** in British Columbia. The rail line also provides a train and bus excursion to **Whitehorse** in the Yukon Territory and provides service for hikers on the **Chilkoot Trail.** All cover the historic route between Skagway and White Pass Summit.

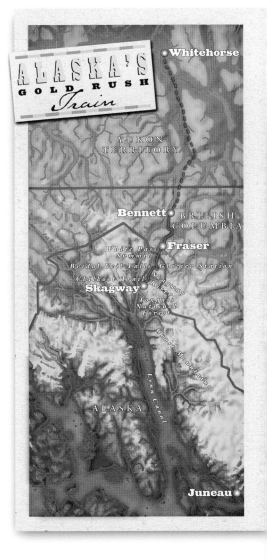

A reminder of how rough this area was at the turn of the century comes just as the train pulls out of Skagway, as it passes the **Gold Rush Cemetery,** where many stampeders are buried. The train then crosses Reid Creek, accelerating on a flat stretch to 25 miles an hour, the top speed on the trip to the summit. The route parallels the Skagway River and after several small bridges, enters a granite corridor along the narrowest part of the canyon. With rocky cliffs on one side and a steep river canyon on the other, it becomes clear why the building of this train is still considered quite a feat of engineering.

The train slows to allow for a good look at **Pitchfork Falls,** a landmark for stampeders. Halfway to the summit is another spectacular waterway—**Bridal Veil Falls.** In the peak runoff season, several dozen water channels can be seen across the valley as the falls cascade into the Skagway River. As the train gains elevation along the steep lines, the crew often advises those who are squeamish about heights to

The doors of the Golden North Hotel in Skagway have been open since the days of the gold rush.

keep their eyes away from the drop to the valley floor far below. After passing through a tunnel, the train pulls its way up to **Inspiration Point** and a spectacular view of the Inside Passage and Skagway, 17 miles below.

The canyon below Inspiration Point is known as **Dead Horse Gulch.** Guides explain how prospectors, desperate for gold, abused their horses and left thousands to die on the trail. Their bones still lie throughout the area, bleaching in the sun. A narrow notch brings the train up to White Pass Summit, elevation 2,865 feet. On a rise to the west, two flags fly throughout the summer to mark the boundary between the United States and Canada. Here the engines are moved from one end to the other, in preparation for the trip back to Skagway. For those traveling farther, other trains continue 8 miles to Fraser, British Columbia, where passengers can board another train bound for Lake Bennett or motor coaches for the trip to Whitehorse.

■ The old steam engines on the route guzzled so much fuel and water that railroaders called them "hogs." It followed naturally that the engineer was called a "hoghead."

■ May of 2000 saw the unveiling of a new Canada Post stamp showcasing the *White Pass & Yukon Route* as one of Canada's famous tourist attractions. The train is featured on the international rate 55-cent stamp, which is the Canada-to-U.S. first-class letter rate.

RATES

The *White Pass & Yukon Route Railway* operates between the beginning of May and the end of September, with the popular trip to the Summit taking about three hours. Rail fare is $78 for adults, $39 for children 3 through 12, and free for infants. (All prices are U.S. dollars.) Reservations are a must. For those wanting a longer journey, the **Lake Bennett Adventure** runs in June, July, and August. The excursion includes viewing the exhibits housed in a restored 1903 station, plus a walking tour during a two-hour layover at Lake Bennett. Along with reservations, proof of citizenship is required on this trip. Fares are $128 for adults, $64 for children.

True train buffs may not be able to pass up the chance to take this excursion when it's led by the vintage Steam Engine No. 73. The *WP&YR* offers this trip, which includes photo run-bys, every Saturday in June, July, and August. Prices are $156 for adults and $78 for children.

The railroad recommends making reservations at least thirty days prior to travel. While there is no penalty for changes, the railroad does charge a ten-percent cancellation fee.

WHAT'S INCLUDED: Summit excursions include a complimentary cold beverage, with snacks available for purchase. The longer

HIGHLIGHT

■ *Ten million dollars of gold spilled out of Skagway into U.S. mints between July and November of 1898. By 1900, another 38 million had been added to the till. Visitors to Skagway today can still experience the excitement of the hunt, tourist-style. Several outfits arrange to take visitors panning for gold. Guides are on hand teaching how to shake a pan filled with dirt and water in hopes of finding a few gold flakes at the bottom. Nuggett Express Goldpanning: (907) 983–3300; Liarsville Gold Rush Trail Camp of 1898: (907) 983–3000; Klondike Dredge Company: (907) 983–3175.*

■ Before the railroad was built, the White Pass could be traveled only by foot with pack animals. More than 3,000 animals died on the trail due to the harsh conditions.

■ The White Pass Summit is one of the steepest railroad grades in the world, climbing 2,865 feet in just 20 miles, making cliff-hanging turns of 16 degrees.

trips to Lake Bennett include a boxed lunch, which comes with a bonus White Pass Railroad lapel pin.

ON BOARD

DINING: Although no food service is offered on board the train, passengers can purchase a selection of simple snacks. The lunch provided on the longer Lake Bennett trip usually includes a turkey croissant sandwich, an apple, chips, and a chocolate bar, all packaged in a souvenir train-shaped box.

DRESS CODE: Comfortable. Weather conditions can vary in a single trip, so dress in layers and include a light rain jacket. Passengers who will be hiking should take care to bring appropriate footwear.

PASSENGERS: Many visitors come as part of an Alaskan cruise. Cruise passengers can purchase their tickets on board their ships, and the railroad provides convenient dockside service. Independent travelers frequently take advantage of the ferry and water taxi service between Haines and Skagway.

CREW: An onboard guide gives a commentary about the history and scenery throughout the trip. Passengers are also given a comprehensive magazine as they board; it is keyed to point-of-interest markers beside the tracks.

Some of the WP&YR's *restored parlor cars are more than one hundred years old.*

Determined railroad workers often had to hang from ropes and hand drill blasting holes to clear away the rock.

■ An estimated 100,000 people made the hard journey to Klondike in the Gold Rush, searching for their fortunes. Many spent an entire year just getting to Alaska.

MAJOR STOPS

■ **SKAGWAY:** After the gold rush ended, the town of Skagway continued to survive as the "gateway to the Yukon," with the *WP&YR* carrying supplies from tidewater to the interior for new settlements. Today, about 800 people live in Skagway, and the town's income is mostly derived from the hundreds of thousands of tourists who come each year to relive gold-rush history. Today, wooden sidewalks, old-fashioned saloons, quaint gift shops, and horse-drawn carriages re-create the times when this small native fishing village was overrun by hordes of prospectors. Skagway has one main street called

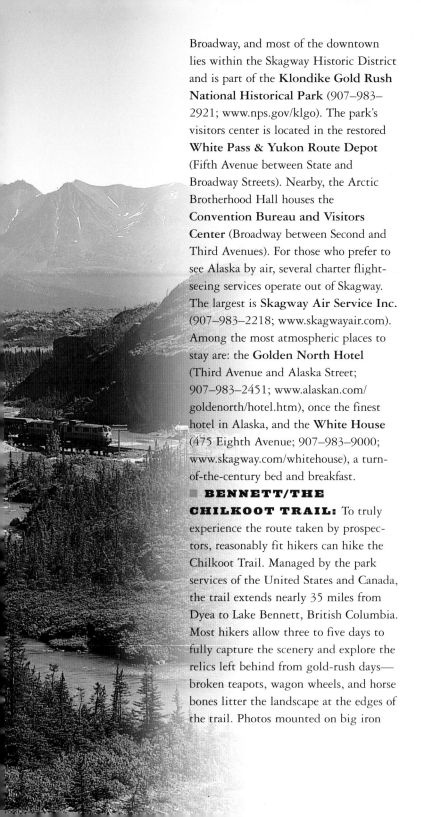

Broadway, and most of the downtown lies within the Skagway Historic District and is part of the **Klondike Gold Rush National Historical Park** (907–983–2921; www.nps.gov/klgo). The park's visitors center is located in the restored **White Pass & Yukon Route Depot** (Fifth Avenue between State and Broadway Streets). Nearby, the Arctic Brotherhood Hall houses the **Convention Bureau and Visitors Center** (Broadway between Second and Third Avenues). For those who prefer to see Alaska by air, several charter flight-seeing services operate out of Skagway. The largest is **Skagway Air Service Inc.** (907–983–2218; www.skagwayair.com). Among the most atmospheric places to stay are: the **Golden North Hotel** (Third Avenue and Alaska Street; 907–983–2451; www.alaskan.com/goldenorth/hotel.htm), once the finest hotel in Alaska, and the **White House** (475 Eighth Avenue; 907–983–9000; www.skagway.com/whitehouse), a turn-of-the-century bed and breakfast.

■ **BENNETT/THE CHILKOOT TRAIL:** To truly experience the route taken by prospectors, reasonably fit hikers can hike the Chilkoot Trail. Managed by the park services of the United States and Canada, the trail extends nearly 35 miles from Dyea to Lake Bennett, British Columbia. Most hikers allow three to five days to fully capture the scenery and explore the relics left behind from gold-rush days—broken teapots, wagon wheels, and horse bones litter the landscape at the edges of the trail. Photos mounted on big iron

■ The distinctive long, yellow streetcars used to tour Skagway were once used for tours in Yellowstone and Yosemite National Parks.

frames show what the trail looked like a hundred years ago. A limited number of permits are available daily to cross the pass: Parks Canada (800–661–0486) is the place to call for information. The *White Pass & Yukon Route Railway* offers transportation from the end of the trail at Bennett back to Skagway, Alaska, or to Fraser, British Columbia.

INFORMATION

■ **White Pass & Yukon Route**, P. O. Box 435, Skagway, AK 99840; (907) 983–2217 or (800) 343–7373. **E-mail:** info@whitepass.net. **Web site:** www.whitepass railroad.com.

■ **Skagway:** www.skagway.org

■ **Gold Rush History:** www.gold-rush.org

Index